The Two Lovers of Heaven: Chrysanthus and Daria
A Drama of Early Christian Rome

Pedro Calderon de la Barca

Contents

PREFATORY NOTE.	10
INTRODUCTION.	17
ACT THE FIRST.	25
ACT THE SECOND.	75
ACT THE THIRD.	131

THE TWO LOVERS OF HEAVEN: CHRYSANTHUS AND DARIA

A DRAMA OF EARLY CHRISTIAN ROME

BY

Pedro Calderon de la Barca

Calderon's Family Motto.

"POR LA FE MORIRE". --

FOR THE FAITH WELCOME DEATH.

THIS motto is taken from the engraved coat of arms prefixed to an historical account of "the very noble and ancient house of Calderon de la Barca"--a rather scarce work which I have never seen alluded to in any account of the poet. The circumstances from which the motto was assigned to the family are given with some minuteness at pp. 56 and 57 of the work referred to. It is enough to mention that the martyr who first used the expression was Don Sancho Ortiz Calderon de la Barca, a Commander of the Order of Santiago. He was in the service of the renowned king, Don Alfonso the Wise, towards the close of the thirteenth century, and having been taken prisoner by the Moors before Gibraltar, he was offered his life on the usual conditions of apostasy. But he refused all overtures, saying: "Pues mi Dios por mi murio, yo quiero morir por el", a phrase which has a singular resemblance to the key note of this drama. Don Ortiz Calderon was eventually put to death with great cruelty, after some alternations of good and bad treatment. See "Descripcion, Armas, Origen, y Descendencia de la muy noble y antigua Casa de Calderon de la Barca", etc., que Escrivio El Rmo. P. M. Fr. Phelipe de la Gandara, etc., Obra Postuma, que saca a luz Juan de

Zuniga. Madrid, 1753.

D. F. M. C.

TO HENRY WADSWORTH LONGFELLOW, IN GRATEFUL RECOLLECTION OF SOME DELIGHTFUL DAYS SPENT WITH HIM AT ROME,

This Drama is dedicated BY DENIS FLORENCE MAC-CARTHY.

TO LONGFELLOW.

I.

PENSIVE within the Colosseum's walls
    I stood with thee, O Poet of the West!--
    The day when each had been a welcome guest
    In San Clemente's venerable halls:--
Ah, with what pride my memory now recalls
    That hour of hours, that flower of all the rest,
    When with thy white beard falling on thy breast--
    That noble head, that well might serve as Paul's
In some divinest vision of the saint
    By Raffael dreamed, I heard thee mourn the dead--
    The martyred host who fearless there, though faint,
Walked the rough road that up to Heaven's gate led:
    These were the pictures Calderon loved to paint

In golden hues that here perchance have fled.

II.

YET take the colder copy from my hand,
    Not for its own but for THE MASTER'S sake,--
    Take it, as thou, returning home, wilt take
    From that divinest soft Italian land
Fixed shadows of the Beautiful and Grand
    In sunless pictures that the sun doth make--
    Reflections that may pleasant memories wake
    Of all that Raffael touched, or Angelo planned:--
As these may keep what memory else might lose,
    So may this photograph of verse impart
    An image, though without the native hues
Of Calderon's fire, and yet with Calderon's art,
    Of what Thou lovest through a kindred Muse
    That sings in heaven, yet nestles in the heart.

D. F. M. C.

Dublin, August 24th, 1869.

PREFATORY NOTE.

THE PROFESSOR OF POETRY AT OXFORD AND THE AUTOS SACRAMENTALES OF CALDERON.

Although the Drama here presented to the public is not an 'Auto,' the present may be a not inappropriate occasion to draw the attention of all candid readers to the remarks of the Professor of Poetry at Oxford on the 'Autos Sacramentales' of Calderon--remarks founded entirely on the volume of translations from these Autos published by me in 1867,[*] although not mentioned by name, as I conceive in fairness it ought to have been, by Sir F. H. Doyle in his printed Lectures.[+]

In his otherwise excellent analysis of The Dream of Gerontius, Sir F. H. Doyle is mistaken as to any direct impression having been made upon the mind of Dr. Newman in reference to it by the Autos of Calderon. So late as March 3, 1867, in thanking me for the volume made use of by Sir F. H. Doyle, Dr. Newman implies that up to that period he had not devoted any particular attention even to this most important and unique development of Spanish religious poetry. The only complete Auto of Calderon that had previously appeared in English--my own translation of The Sorceries of Sin, had, indeed, been in his hands from 1859, and I wish I could flatter myself that it had in any way led to the production of a master-piece like The Dream of Gerontius. But I cannot indulge that delusion. Dr. Newman had internally and externally too many sources of inspiration to necessitate an adoption even of such high models as the Spanish Autos. Besides, The Dream of Gerontius is no more an Auto than Paradise Lost, or the Divina Commedia. In these, only real personages, spiritual and material, are represented, or monsters that typified human passions, but did not personify them. In the Autos it is precisely the reverse. Rarely do actual beings take part in the drama, and then only as personifications of the predominant vices or passions of the individuals whose names they bear. Thus in my own volume, Belshazzar is not treated so much as an historical character, but rather as the personification of the pride and haughtiness of a voluptuous king. In The Divine Philothea, in the same volume, there are no actual beings whatever, except The Prince of Light and The Prince of Darkness or The Demon. In truth, there is nothing analogous to a Spanish Auto in English original poetry. The nearest approach to it, and the only one, is The Prometheus Unbound of Shelley. There, indeed, The Earth, Ocean, The Spirits of the Hours, The Phantasm of Jupiter, Demogorgon, and Prometheus himself, read like the 'Personas' of a Spanish Auto, and the poetry is worthy the resemblance. The Autos Sacramentales differ also, not only in degree but in kind from every form of Mystery or Morality produced either in England or on the Continent. But to return to the lecture by Sir F. H. Doyle. Even in smaller matters he is not accurate. Thus he has transcribed incorrectly from my Introduction the name of the distinguished commentator on the Autos of Calderon and their translator into German--Dr. Lorinser. This Sir F. H. Doyle has printed throughout his lecture 'Lorinzer'. From private letters which I have had the honour of receiving from this learned writer, there can be no doubt that the form as originally given by me is the right one. With these corrections the lecture of Sir F. H. Doyle may be quoted as a valuable testimony to the extraordinary poetic beauty of these Autos even in a translation.

LECTURE III.--Dr. Newman's Dream of Gerontius.

"It is probable, indeed, that the first idea of composing such a dramatic work may have been suggested to Dr. Newman by the Autos Sacramentales of Spain, and especially by those of the illustrious Calderon; but, so far as I can learn, he has derived hardly anything from them beyond the vaguest hints, except, indeed, the all-important knowledge, that a profound religious feeling can represent itself, and that effectively, in the outward form of a play. I may remark that these Spanish Autos of Calderon constitute beyond all question a very wonderful and a very original school of poetry, and I am not without hope that, when I know my business a little better, we may examine them impartially together. Nay, even as it is, Calderon stands so indisputably at the head of all Catholic religious dramatists, among whom Dr. Newman has recently enrolled himself, that perhaps it may not be out of place to inquire for a moment into his poetical methods and aims, in order that we may then discover, if we can, how and why the disciple differs from his master. Now there is a great conflict of opinion as to the precise degree of merit which these particular Spanish dramas possess. Speaking as an ignorant man, I should say, whilst those who disparage them seem rather hasty in their judgments, and not so well informed as could be wished, still the kind of praise which they receive from their most enthusiastic admirers puzzles and does not instruct us.

"Taking for example, the great German authority on this point, Dr. Lorinzer [Lorinser], as our guide, we see his poet looming dimly through a cloud of incense, which may embalm his memory, but certainly does not improve our eyesight. Indeed, according to him, any appreciation of Calderon is not to be dreamt of by a Protestant". Lectures, pp. 109, 110.

With every respect for Sir F. H. Doyle, Dr. Lorinser says no such thing. He was too well informed of what had been done in Germany on the same subject, before he himself undertook the formidable task of attempting a complete translation of all the Autos of Calderon, to have fallen into such an error. Cardinal Diepenbrock, Archbishop of Breslau, who, in his "Das Leben ein Traum" (an Auto quite distinct from the well known drama "La Vida es Sueno") first commenced this interesting labour in Germany, was of course a Catholic. But Eichendorff and Braunfels, who both preceded Dr. Lorinser, were Protestants. Augustus Schlegel and Baron von Schack, who have written so profoundly and so truly on the Autos, are expressly referred to by Dr. Lorinser, and it is superfluous to say that they too were Protestants. Sir F. H. Doyle, in using my translation of the passage which will presently be quoted, changes the word 'thoroughly' into 'properly', as if it were a more correct rendering of the original. Unfortunately, however, there is nothing to represent either word in the German. Dr. Lorinser says, that by many, not by all, Calderon cannot be enjoyed as much as he deserves, because a great number of persons best competent to judge of his merits are deficient in the knowledge of Catholic faith and Catholic theology which for the understanding of Calderon is indispensible--"welche fuer Calderons Verstaendniss unerlaesslich ist". Sir F. H. Doyle says that to him these Autos are not "incomprehensible at all" (p. 112), but then he understands them all the better for being a scholar and a churchman.

Sir F. H. Doyle thus continues his reference to Dr. Lorinser. "Even learned critics", he says, "highly cultivated in all the niceties of aesthetics, are deficient in the knowledge of Catholic faith and Catholic theology properly to understand Calderon" (Lectures, p. 110, taken from the Introduction to my volume, p. 3). "Old traditions", continues Dr. Lorinzer, "which twine round the dogma like a beautiful garland of legends, deeply profound thoughts expressed here and there by some of the Fathers of the Church, are made use of with such incredible skill and introduced so appositely at the right place, that . . . . frequently it is not easy to guess the source from whence they have been derived" (Lectures, p. 111, taken from the Introduction to my volume, p. 6).

This surely is unquestionably true, and the argument used by Sir F. H. Doyle to controvert it does not go for much. These Autos, no doubt, were, as he says, "composed in the first instance to gratify, and did gratify, the uneducated populace of Madrid". Yes, the crowds that listened delighted and entranced to these wonderful compositions, were, for the most part, "uneducated" in the ordinary meaning of that word. But in the special education necessary for their thorough enjoyment, the case was very different. It is not too much to say that, as the result of Catholic training, teaching, intuition, and association, the least instructed of his Madrid audience more easily understood Calderon's allusions, than the great majority of those who, reared up in totally different ideas, are able to do, even after much labour and sometimes with considerable sympathy. Mr. Tennyson says that he counts--

"The gray barbarian lower than the Christian child",

because the almost intuitive perceptions of a Christian child as to the nature of God and the truths of Revelation, place it intellectually higher than even the mature intelligence of a savage. I mean no disrespect to Sir F. H. Doyle, but I think that Calderon would have found at Madrid in the middle of the seventeenth century, and would find there to-day, in a Catholic boy of fifteen, a more intelligent and a better instructed critic on these points, than even the learned professor himself. I shall make no further comments on Sir F. H. Doyle's Lecture, but give his remarks on Calderon's Autos to the end.

"At the same time", says Sir F. H. Doyle, "Dr. Lorinzer's knowledge of his subject is so profound, and his appreciation of his favourite author so keen, that for me, who am almost entirely unacquainted with this branch of literature, formally to oppose his views, would be an act of presumption, of which I am, as I trust, incapable. I may, however, perhaps be permitted to observe, that with regard to the few pieces of this kind which in an English dress I have read, whilst I think them not only most ingenious but also surprisingly beautiful, they do not strike me as incomprehensible at all. We must accept them, of course, as coming from the mind of a devout Catholic and Spanish gentleman, who belongs to the seventeenth century; but when once that is agreed upon, there are no difficulties greater than those which we might expect to find in any system of poetry so remote from our English habits of thought. There is, for instance, the Divine Philothea, in other words, our human spirit considered as the destined bride of Christ. This sacred drama, we may well call it the swan-song of Calderon's extreme old age, is steeped throughout in a serene power and a mellow beauty of style, making it not unworthy to be ranked with that Oedipus Colonaeus which glorified the sun-set of his illustrious predecessor: but yet, Protestant as I am, I cannot discover that it is in the least obscure. Faith, Hope, Charity, the Five Senses, Heresy, Judaism, Paganism, Atheism, and the like, which in inferior hands must have been mere lay figures, are there instinct with a dramatic life and energy such as beforehand I could hardly have supposed possible. Moreover, in spite of Dr. Lorinzer's odd encomiums, each allegory as it rises is more neatly rounded off, and shows a finer grain, than any of the personifications of Spenser; so that the religious effect and the theological effect intended by the writer, are both amply produced--yes, produced upon us, his heretical admirers. Hence, even if there be mysterious treasures of beauty below the surface, to which we aliens must remain blind for ever, this expression, which broke from the lips of one to whom I was eagerly reading [Mr. Mac-Carthy's translation of] the play, 'Why, in the original this must be as grand as Dante', tends to show that such merits as do come within our ken are not likely to be thrown away upon any fair-minded Protestant. Dr. Newman, as a Catholic, will have entered, I presume, more deeply still into the spirit of these extraordinary creations; his life, however, belongs to a different era and to a colder people. And thus, however much he may have been directed to the choice of a subject by the old Mysteries and Moralities (of which these Spanish Autos must be taken as the final development and bright consummate flower), he has treated that subject, when once undertaken by him, entirely from his own point of view. 'Gerontius' is meant to be studied and dwelt upon by the meditative reader. The Autos of Calderon were got ready by perhaps the most accomplished playwright that ever lived, to amuse and stimulate a thronging southern population. 'Gerontius' is, we may perhaps say for Dr. Newman in the words of Shelley,

'The voice of his own soul
Heard in the calm of thought';

whilst the conceptions of the Spanish dramatist burst into life with tumultuous music, gorgeous scenery, and all the pomp and splendour of the Catholic Church. No wonder therefore that our English Auto, though composed with the same genuine purpose of using verse, and dramatic verse, to promote a religious and even a theological end, should differ from them in essence as well as in form. There is room however for both kinds in the wide empire of Poetry, and though Dr. Newman himself would be the first to cry shame upon me if I were to name him with Calderon even for a moment, still his Mystery of this most unmysterious age will, I believe, keep its honourable place in our English literature as an impressive, an attractive, and an original production"--pp. 109, 115.

I may mention that the volume containing Belshazzar's Feast, and The Divine Philothea, the Auto particularly referred to by Sir F. H. Doyle, has been called Mysteries of Corpus Christi by the publisher. A not inappropriate title, it would seem, from the last observations of the distinguished Professor. A third Auto, The Sorceries of Sin, is given in my Three Plays of Calderon, now on sale by Mr. B. Quaritch, 15 Piccadilly, London. The Divine Philothea, The Sorceries of Sin, and Belshazzar's Feast are the only Autos of Calderon that have ever been translated either fully, or, with one exception, even partially into English.

D. F. MAC-CARTHY.
74 Upper Gardiner Street, Dublin,
March 1, 1870.

* AUTOS SACRAMENTALES: THE DIVINE PHILOTHEA: BELSHAZZAR'S FEAST. Two
Autos, from the Spanish of Calderon. With a Commentary from the German
of Dr. Franz Lorinser. By Denis Florence Mac-Carthy, M.R.I.A. Dublin:
James Duffy, 15 Wellington Quay, and 22 Paternoster Row, London.

+ LECTURES DELIVERED BEFORE THE UNIVERSITY OF OXFORD, 1868. By Sir F.
H. Doyle Bart., M.A., B.C L., Late Fellow of All Souls', Professor of
Poetry. London: Macmillan & Co., 1869.

THE TWO LOVERS OF HEAVEN.[1]

INTRODUCTION.

IN the "Teatro escogido de Don Pedro Calderon de la Barca" (1868), at present in course of publication by the Royal Academy of Madrid, Calderon's dramas, exclusive of the autos sacramentales, which do not form a part of the collection, are divided into eight classes. The seventh of these comprises what the editor calls mystical dramas, and those founded on the Legends or the Lives of Saints. The eighth contains the philosophical or purely ideal dramas. This last division, in which the editor evidently thinks the genius of Calderon attained its highest development, at least as far as the secular theatre is concerned, contains but two dramas, The Wonder-working Magician, and

Life's a Dream. The mystical dramas, which form the seventh division, are more numerous, but of these five are at present known to us only by name. Those that remain are Day-break in Copacabana, The Chains of the Demon, The Devotion of the Cross, The Purgatory of St. Patrick, The Sibyl of the East, The Virgin of the Sanctuary, and The Two Lovers of Heaven. The editor, Sr. D. P. De La Escosura, seems to think it necessary to offer some apology for not including The Two Lovers of Heaven among the philosophical instead of the mystical dramas. He says: "There is a great analogy and, perhaps, resemblance between "El Magico Prodigioso" (The Wonder-working Magician), and "Los dos amantes del cielo" (The Two Lovers of Heaven); but in the second, as it seems to us, the purely mystical predominates in such a manner over the philosophical, that it does not admit of its being classified in the same group as the first (El Magico Prodigioso), and La Vida es Sueno (Life's a Dream)". Introduccion, p. cxxxvii. note. Whether this distinction is well founded or not it is unnecessary to determine. It is sufficient for our purpose that it establishes the high position among the greatest plays of Calderon of the drama which is here presented to the English reader in the peculiar and always difficult versification of the original. Whether less philosophical or more mystical than The Wonder-working Magician, The Two Lovers of Heaven possesses a charm of its own in which its more famous rival seems deficient. In the admirable "Essay on the Genius of Calderon" (ch. ii. p. 34), with which Archbishop Trench introduces his spirited analysis of La Vida es Sueno, he refers to the group of dramas which forms, with one exception, the seventh and eighth divisions of the classification above referred to, and pays a just tribute to the superior merits of Los dos amantes del cielo. After alluding to the dramas, the argument of which is drawn from the Old Testament, and especially to The Locks of Absalom, which he considers the noblest specimen, he continues: "Still more have to do with the heroic martyrdoms and other legends of Christian antiquity, the victories of the Cross of Christ over all the fleshly and spiritual wickednesses of the ancient heathen world. To this theme, which is one almost undrawn upon in our Elizabethan drama,--Massinger's Virgin Martyr is the only example I remember,--he returns continually, and he has elaborated these plays with peculiar care. Of these The Wonder-working Magician is most celebrated; but others, as The Joseph of Women, The Two Lovers of Heaven, quite deserve to be placed on a level, if not higher than it. A tender pathetic grace is shed over this last, which gives it a peculiar charm. Then too he has occupied what one might venture to call the region of sacred mythology, as in The Sibyl of the East, in which the profound legends identifying the Cross of Calvary and the Tree of Life are wrought up into a poem of surpassing beauty".[2] An excellent German version of Los dos amantes del cielo is to be found in the second volume of the "Spanisches Theater", by Schack, whose important work on Dramatic Art and Literature in Spain, is still untranslated into the language of that country,--a singular neglect, when his later and less elaborate work, "Poesie and Kunst der Araber in Spanien und Sicilien" (Berlin, 1865), has already found an excellent Spanish interpreter in Don Juan Valera, two volumes of whose "Poesia y Arte de los Arabes en Espana y Sicilia" (Madrid, 1868), I was fortunate enough to meet with during a recent visit to Spain.

The story of SS. Chrysanthus and Daria (The Two Lovers of Heaven), whose martyrdom took place at Rome A.D. 284, and whose festival occurs on the 25th of October, is to be found in a very abridged form in the "Legenda Aurea" of Jacobus de Voragine, c. 152. The fullest account, and that which Calderon had evidently before him when writing The Two Lovers of Heaven, is given by Surius in his great work, "De Probatis Sanctorum Vitis", October, p. 378. This history is referred to by Villegas at the conclusion of his own condensed narrative in the following passage, which I take from the old English version of his Lives of Saints, by John Heigham, anno 1630.

"The Church doth celebrate the feast of SS. Chrisanthus and Daria, the 25th of October, and their death was in the year of our Lord God 284, in the raigne of Numerianus, Emperor. The martyrdom of these saints was written by Verinus and Armenius, priests of St. Stephen, Pope and Martyr: Metaphrastes enlarged it somewhat more. St. Damasus made certain eloquent verses in praise of these saints, and set them on their tombe. There is mention of them also in the Romaine Martirologe, and in that of Usuardus: as also in the 5. tome of Surius; in Cardinal Baronius, and Gregory of Turonensis", p. 849.

A different abridgment of the story as given by Surius, is to be found in Ribadeneyra's "Flos Sanctorum" (the edition before me being that of Barcelona, 1790, t. 3. p. 304). It concludes with the same list of authorities, which, however, is given with more precision. The old English translation by W. P. Esq., second edition: London, 1730, p. 369, gives them thus:

"Surius in his fifth tome, and Cardinal Baronius in his 'Annotations upon the Martyrologies', and in the second tome of his Annals, and St. Gregory of Tours in his 'Book of the Glory of the Martyrs', make mention of the Saints Chrysanthus and Daria".

The following is taken from Caxton's Golden Legende, or translation of the Legenda Aurea of Jacobus de Voragine. I have transcribed from the following edition, which is thus described in the Colophon:

"The legende named in latyn Legenda Aurea, that is to say in englyshe the golden legende, For lyke as golde passeth all other metalles, so this boke excedeth all other bokes". "Finyshed the xxvii daye of August, the yere of our lord M. CCCCC. XXVII, the xix yere of the regne of our souverayne lord Kynge Henry the eyght. Imprynted at London in Flete Strete at the Sygne of the Sonne by Wynkyn de Worde".

In the following extract the spelling is somewhat modernised, and a few obsolete words are omitted.

"The Life of Saynt Crysant and Saynte Daria".
    Fo. cc. lxxxv.

"Here followeth the lyfe of Saynt Crysaunt, and fyrst of his name. And of Saynte Daria, and of her name.

"Of Crysaunt is said as growen and multyplyed of God. For when his father would have made hym do sacrifyce to the idols, God gave to hym force and power to contrary and gaynsay his father, and yield himself to God. Daria is sayd of dare to give, for she gave her to two thynges. Fyrst will to do evil, when she had will to draw Crysaunt to sacrifyce to the idols. And after she gave her to good will when Crysaunt had converted her to Almighty God.

"Crysaunt was son of a ryght noble man that was named Polymne. And when his father saw that his son was taught in the faith of Jesu Chryst, and that he could not withdraw him therefrom, and make him do sacrifyce to the idols, he commanded that he should be closed in a stronge hold and put to hym five maidens for to seduce him with blandyshynge and fayre wordes. And when he had prayed God that he should not be surmounted with no fleshly desyre, anon these maydens were so overcome with slepe, that they myght not take neither meat ne drinke as long as they were there, but as soon as they were out, they took both meat and drinke. And one Daria, a noble and wise virgin of the goddess Vesta, arrayed her nobly with clothes as she had been a goddess, and prayed that she myght be letten enter in to Crysant and that she would restore him to the idols and to his father. And when she was come in, Crysant reproved her of the pride of her vesture. And she answered that she had not done it for pride but for to draw him to do sacrifyce to the idols and restore him to his father. And then Crysant reproved her because she worshipped them as gods. For they had been in their times evil and sinners. And Daria answered, the philosophers called the elements by the names of men. And Crysant said to her, if one worship the earth as a goddess, and another work and labour the earth as a churl or ploughman, to whom giveth the earth most? It is plain that it giveth more to the ploughman than to him that worshippeth it. And in like wise he said of the sea and of the other elements. And then Crysant and Daria converted to him, coupled them together by the grace of the Holy Ghost, and feigned to be joined by carnal marriage, and converted many others to our Lord. For Claudian, who had been one of their persecutors, they converted to the faith of our Lord, with his wife and children and many other knights. And after this Crysant was enclosed in a stinking prison by the commandment of Numerian, but the stink turned anon into a right sweet odour and savour. And Daria was brought to the bordel, but a lion that was in the amphitheatre came and kept the door of the bordel. And then there was sent thither a man to befoul and corrupt the virgin, but anon he was taken by the lion, and the lion began to look at the virgin like as he demanded what he should do with the caitiff. And the virgin commanded that he should do him no hurt but let him go. And anon he was converted and ran through the city, and began to cry that Daria was a goddess. And then hunters were sent thither to take the lion. And they anon fell down at the feet of the virgin and were converted by her. And then the provost commanded them to make a great fire within the entrance of the bordel, so that the lion should be brent with Daria. And the lion considering this thing, felt dread, and roaring took leave of the virgin, and went whither he would without hurting of any body. And when the provost had done to Crysant and Daria many diverse torments, and might not grieve them, at the last they without compassion were put in a deep pit, and earth and stones thrown on them. And so were consecrated martyrs of Christ".

With regard to the exact year in which the martyrdom of SS. Chrysanthus and Daria took place, it may be mentioned that in the valuable "Vies des Saints", Paris, 1701 (republished in 1739), where the whole legend undergoes a very critical examination, the generally received date, A.D.

284, is considered erroneous. The reign of the emperor Numerianus (A.D. 283-284), in which it is alleged to have occurred, lasted but eight months, during which period no persecution of the Christians is recorded. The writer in the work just quoted (Adrien Baillet) conjectures that the martyrdom of these saints took place in the reign of Valerian, and not later than the month of August, 257, "s' il est vray que le pape Saint Etienne qui mourut alois avoit donne ordre qu' on recueillit les actes de leur martyre"--Les Vies des Saints, Paris, 1739, t. vii. p. 385.

1. Los dos amantes del cielo: Crisanto y Daria. Comedias de Don Pedro Calderon de la Barca. Por Don Juan Eugenio Hartzenbusch. Madrid, 1865, tomo 3, p. 234.

2. It may be added to what Dr. Trench has so well said, that Calderon's auto, "El arbol del mejor Fruto" (The Tree of the choicest Fruit), is founded on the same sublime theme. It is translated into German by Lorinser, under the title of "Der Baum der bessern Frucht", Breslau, 1861.

THE TWO LOVERS OF HEAVEN.

PERSONS.

NUMERIANUS, Emperor of Rome.
POLEMIUS, Chief Senator.
CHRYSANTHUS, his son.
CLAUDIUS, cousin of Chrysanthus.
AURELIUS, a Roman general.
CARPOPHORUS, a venerable priest.
ESCARPIN, servant of Chrysanthus.
DARIA,
CYNTHIA,
NISIDA,
CHLORIS,
        } Priestesses of Diana. Two spirits. Angels.
         Soldiers, servants, people, music, etc.

SCENE: Rome and its environs.

ACT THE FIRST.

SCENE I.--A Room in the house of Polemius at Rome.

Chrysanthus is seen seated near a writing table on which are several books: he is reading a small volume with deep attention.

CHRYSANTHUS.
Ah! how shallow is my mind!
How confined! and how restricted![3]
Ah! how driftless are my words!
And my thoughts themselves how driftless!
Since I cannot comprehend,
Cannot pierce the secrets hidden
In this little book that I
Found by chance with others mingled.
I its meaning cannot reach,
Howsoe'er my mind I rivet,
Though to this, and this alone,
Many a day has now been given.
But I cannot therefore yield,

Must not own myself outwitted:--
No; a studious toil so great
Should not end in aught so little.
O'er this book my whole life long
Shall I brood until the riddle
Is made plain, or till some sage
Simplifies what here is written.
For which end I 'll read once more
Its beginning. How my instinct
Uses the same word with which
Even the book itself beginneth!--
"In the beginning was the Word" . .[4]
If in language plain and simple
Word means speech, how then was it
In the beginning? Since a whisper
Presupposes power to breathe it,
Proves an earlier existence,
And to that anterior Power
Here the book doth not bear witness.
Then this follows: "And the Word
Was with God"--nay more, 't is written,
"And the Word was God: was with Him
In the beginning, and by HIM then
All created things were made
And without Him naught was finshed":--
Oh! what mysteries, what wonders,
In this tangled labyrinthine
Maze lie hid! which I so many
Years have studied, with such mingled
Aid from lore divine and human
Have in vain tried to unriddle!--
"In the beginning was the Word".--
Yes, but when was this beginning?

Was it when Jove, Neptune, Pluto
Shared the triple zones betwixt them,
When the one took to himself
Heaven supreme, one hell's abysses,
And the sea the third, to Ceres
Leaving earth, the ever-wing`ed
Time to Saturn, fire to Phoebus,
And the air to Jove's great sister?[5]--
No, it could not have been then,
For the fact of their partition
Shows that heaven and earth then were,
Shows that sea and land existed:--
The beginning then must be
Something more remote and distant:
He who has expressly said
'The beginning,' must have hinted
At the primal cause of all things,
At the first and great beginning,
All things growing out of HIM,
He himself the pre-existent:--
Yes, but then a new beginning
Must we seek for this beginner,
And so on ad infinitum;
Since if I, on soaring pinion
Seek from facts to rise to causes,
Rising still from where I had risen,
I will find at length there is
No beginning to the beginning,
And the inference that time
Somehow was, ere time existed,
And that that which ne'er begun
Ne'er can end, is plain and simple.
But, my thought, remain not here,

Rest not in those narrow limits,
But rise up with me and dare
Heights that make the brain grow dizzy:--
And at once to enter there,
Other things being pretermitted,
Let us venture where the mind,
As the darkness round it thickens,
Almost faints as we resume
What this mystic scribe has written.
"And the Word", this writer says,
"Was made flesh!" Ah! how can this be?
Could the Word that in the beginning
Was with God, was God, was gifted
With such power as to make all things,
Could it be made flesh? In pity,
Heavens! or take from me at once
All the sense that you have given me,
Or at once on me bestow
Some intelligence, some glimmer
Of clear light through these dark shadows:--
Deity, unknown and hidden,
God or Word, whate'er thou beest,
Of Thyself the great beginner,
Of Thyself the end, if, Thou
Being Thyself beyond time's sickle,
Still in time the world didst fashion,
If Thou 'rt life, O living spirit,
If Thou 'rt light, my darkened senses
With Thy life and light enkindle!--
(The voices of two spirits are heard from within, one at each side.)

First Voice.
Hear, Chrysanthus . . .

The Two Lovers of Heaven: Chrysanthus and Daria

Second Voice.
>Listen . . .

CHRYSANTHUS.
>Two
Voices, if they are not instincts,
Shadows without soul or body,
Which my fancy forms within me,
Are contending in my bosom
Each with each at the same instant.
(*Two figures appear on high, one clothed in a dark robe dotted with stars; the other in a bright and beautiful mantle: Chrysanthus does not see them, but in the following scene ever speaks to himself.*)

First Voice.
What this crabbed text here meaneth
By the Word, is plain and simple,
It is Jove to whose great voice
Gods and men obedient listen.

CHRYSANTHUS.
Jove, it must be Jove, by whom
Breath, speech, life itself are given.

Second Voice.
What the holy Gospel means
By the Word, is that great Spirit
Who was in Himself for ever,
First, last, always self-existent.

CHRYSANTHUS.
Self-existent! first and last!

Reason cannot grasp that dictum.

First Voice.
In the beginning of the world
Jove in heaven his high throne fix`ed,
Leaving less imperial thrones
To the other gods to fill them.

CHRYSANTHUS.
Yes, if he could not alone
Rule creation unassisted.

Second Voice.
God was God, long, long before
Earth or heaven's blue vault existed,
He was in Himself, ere He
Gave to time its life and mission.

First Voice.
Worship only pay to Jove,
God o'er all our gods uplifted.

Second Voice.
Worship pay to God alone,
He the infinite, the omniscient.

First Voice.
He doth lord the world below.

Second Voice.
He is Lord of Heaven's high kingdom.

First Voice.

Shun the lightnings of his wrath.

Second Voice.
Seek the waves of his forgiveness. [The Figures disappear.

CHRYSANTHUS.
Oh! what darkness, what confusion,
In myself I find here pitted
'Gainst each other! Spirits twain
Struggle desperately within me,
Spirits twain of good and ill,--
One with gentle impulse wins me
To believe, but, oh! the other
With opposing force resistless
Drives me back to doubt: Oh! who
Will dispel these doubts that fill me?

POLEMIUS (within).
Yes, Carpophorus must pay
For the trouble that this gives me.--

CHRYSANTHUS.
Though these words by chance were spoken
As an omen I 'll admit them:
Since Carpophorus (who in Rome
Was the most renowned, most gifted
Master in all science), now
Flying from the emperor's lictors,
Through suspect of being a Christian,
In lone deserts wild and dismal
Lives a saintly savage life,
He will give to all my wishes
The solution of these doubts:--

And till then, O restless thinking
Torture me and tease no more!
Let me live for that! [His voice gradually rises.

ESCARPIN (within).
      Within there
My young master calls.

CLAUDIUS (within).
      All enter.
(Enter Polemius, Claudius, Aurelius, and Escarpin).

POLEMIUS.
My Chrysanthus, what afflicts thee?

CHRYSANTHUS.
Canst thou have been here, my father?

POLEMIUS.
No, my son, 't was but this instant
That I entered here, alarmed
By the strange and sudden shrillness
Of thy voice; and though I had
On my hands important business,
Grave and weighty, since to me
Hath the Emperor transmitted
This decree, which bids me search
Through the mountains for the Christians
Hidden there, and specially
For Carpophorus, their admitted
Chief and teacher, for which cause
I my voice too thus uplifted--
"Yes, Carpophorus must pay

For the trouble that this gives me"--
I left all at hearing thee.--
Why so absent? so bewildered?
What 's the reason?

CHRYSANTHUS.
    Sir, 't is naught.

POLEMIUS.
Whom didst thou address?

CHRYSANTHUS.
    Here sitting
I was reading to myself,
And perchance conceived some image
I may have addressed in words
Which have from my memory flitted.

POLEMIUS.
The grave sadness that o'erwhelms thee
Will, unless it be resisted,
Undermine thy understanding,
If thou hast it still within thee.

CLAUDIUS.
'T is a loud soliloquy,
'T is a rather audible whisper
That compels one's friends to hasten
Full of fear to his assistance!

CHRYSANTHUS.
Well, excitement may . . .

POLEMIUS.
>   Oh! cease;
That excuse will scarce acquit thee,
Since when one 's alone, excitement
Is a flame that 's seldom kindled.
I am pleased, well pleased to see thee
To the love of books addicted,
But then application should not
To extremes like this be driven,
Nor should letters alienate thee
From thy country, friends, and kinsmen.

CLAUDIUS.
A young man by heaven so favoured,
With such rare endowments gifted,
Blessed with noble birth and valour,
Dowered with genius, rank, and riches,
Can he yield to such enthralment,
Can he make his room a prison,
Can he waste in idle reading
The fair flower of his existence?

POLEMIUS.
Dost thou not remember also
That thou art my son? Bethink thee
That the great Numerianus,
Our good emperor, has given me
The grand government of Rome
As chief senator of the city,
And with that imperial burden
The whole world too--all the kingdoms,
All the provinces subjected
To its varied, vast dominion.

Know'st thou not, from Alexandria,
From my native land, my birth-place,
Where on many a proud escutcheon
My ancestral fame is written,
That he brought me here, the weight
Of his great crown to bear with him,
And that Rome upon my entry
Gave to me a recognition
That repaid the debt it owed me,
Since the victories were admitted
Which in glorious alternation
By my sword and pen were given her?
Through what vanity, what folly,
Wilt thou not enjoy thy birth-right
As my son and heir, indulging
Solely in these idle whimseys?--

CHRYSANTHUS.
Sir, the state in which you see me,
This secluded room, this stillness,
Do not spring from want of feeling,
Or indifference to your wishes.
'T is my natural disposition;
For I have no taste to mingle
In the vulgar vain pursuits
Of the courtier crowds ambitious.
And if living to myself here
More of true enjoyment gives me,
Why would you desire me seek for
That which must my joys diminish?
Let this time of sadness pass,
Let these hours of lonely vigil,
Then for fame and its applauses,

Which no merit of my own,
But my father's name may bring me.

POLEMIUS.
Would it not, my son, be fitter
That you should enjoy those plaudits
In the fresh and blooming spring-time
Of your life, and to hereafter
Leave the loneliness and vigil?

ESCARPIN.
Let me tell a little story
Which will make the whole thing simple:--
A bad painter bought a house,
Altogether a bad business,
For the house itself was bad:
He however was quite smitten
With his purchase, and would show it
To a friend of his, keen-witted,
But bad also: when they entered,
The first room was like a kitchen,
Black and bad:--"This room, you see, sir,
Now is bad, but just permit me
First to have it whitewashed over,
Then shall my own hand with pictures
Paint the walls from floor to ceiling,
Then you 'll see how bright 't will glisten".--
To him thus his friend made answer,
Smiling archly: "Yes, 't will glisten,
But if you would paint it first,
And then whitewash o'er the pictures,
The effect would be much better".--
Now 's the time for you, my lord,

To lay on the shining pigment:
On that brilliant ground hereafter
Will the whitewash fall more fitly,
For, in fine, the poorest painting
Is improved by time's slow finger.

CHRYSANTHUS.
Sir, I say, that in obedience
To your precepts, to your wishes,
I will strive from this day forward
So to act, that you will think me
Changed into another being. [Exit.

POLEMIUS.
Claudius, my paternal instinct
Makes me fear Chrysanthus' sadness,
Makes we tremble that its issue
May result in total madness.
Since thou art his friend and kinsman
Both combined, make out, I pray thee,
What occasions this bewitchment,
To the end that I may break it:
And my promise now I give thee,
That although I should discover
Love's delirious dream delicious
May be at the root,--most likely
At his age the true suspicion,--
It shall not disturb or grieve me.
Nay, since I am doomed to witness
His dejection, it will glad me
To find out that so it springeth.

ESCARPIN.

Once a high priest of Apollo
Had two nephews soft and silly,
More than silly, wretched creatures,
More than wretched, doltish drivels;
And perceiving from experience
How love smartens up its victims,
He but said to them this only,
"Fall in love at least, ye ninnies".--
Thus, though not in love, sir, now,
I 'll be bound he 'll be so quickly,
Merely to oblige you.

POLEMIUS.
     This
Is not quite as I would wish it,
For when anything has happened,
The desire to know it, differs
From the wish it so should happen.

CLAUDIUS.
I, my lord, my best assistance
Offer thee to strive and fathom
From what cause can have arisen
Such dejection and such sadness;
This henceforth shall be my business
To divert him and distract him.

POLEMIUS.
Such precisely are my wishes:
And since now I am forced to go
In obedience to the mission
Sent me by Numerianus,
'Mid the wastes to search for Christians,

In my absence, Claudius,
Most consoling thoughts 't will give me,
To remember that thou watchest
O'er Chrysanthus.

CLAUDIUS.
    From this instant
Until thy return, I promise
Not to leave his side.

POLEMIUS.
    Aurelius . . .

AURELIUS.
My good lord.

POLEMIUS.
    Art sure thou knowest
In this mountain the well-hidden
Cave wherein Carpophorus dwelleth?

AURELIUS.
Him I promise to deliver
To thy hands.

POLEMIUS.
    Then lead the soldiers
Stealthily and with all quickness
To the spot, for all must perish
Who are there found hiding with him:--
For the care with which, ye Heavens!
I uphold the true religion
Of the gods, their faith and worship,

For the zeal that I exhibit
In thus crushing Christ's new law,
Which I hate with every instinct
Of my soul, oh! grant my guerdon
In the cure of my son's illness! [*Exeunt Polemius and Aurelius.*

CLAUDIUS (*to Escarpin*).
Go and tell my lord Chrysanthus
That I wish he would come with me
Forth to-day for relaxation.

ESCARPIN.
Relaxation! just say whither
Are we to go forth to get it;
Of that comfort I get little--

CLAUDIUS.
Outside Rome, Diana's temple
On the Salarian way uplifteth
Its majestic front: the fairest
Of our Roman maids dwell in it:
'T is the custom, as thou knowest,
That the loveliest of Rome's children
Whom patrician blood ennobles,
From their tender years go thither
To be priestesses of the goddess,
Living there till 't is permitted
They should marry: 't is the centre
Of all charms, the magic circle
Drawn around a land of beauty--
Home of deities--Elysium!--
And as great Diana is
Goddess of the groves, her children

Have to her an altar raised
In the loveliest cool green thicket.
Thither, when the evening falleth,
And the season is propitious,
Various squadrons of fair nymphs
Hasten: and it is permitted
Gallant youths, unmarried also,
As an escort to go with them.
There this evening will I lead him.

ESCARPIN.
Well, I doubt that your prescription
Is the best: for fair recluses,
Whose sublime pursuits, restricted
To celestial things, make even
The most innocent thought seem wicked,
Are by no means likely persons
To divert a man afflicted
With this melancholy madness:
Better take him into the thickest
Throng of Rome, there flesh and bone
Goddesses he 'll find, and fitter.--

CLAUDIUS.
Ah! you speak but as the vulgar:
Is it not the bliss of blisses
To adore some lovely being
In the ideal, in the distance,
Almost as a vision?--

ESCARPIN.
    Yes;
'T is delightful; I admit it,

But there 's good and better: think
Of the choice that once a simple
Mother gave her son: she said:
"Egg or rasher, which will I give thee?"
And he said: "The rasher, mother,
But with the egg upon it, prithee".
"Both are best", so says the proverb.

CLAUDIUS.
Well, if tastes did n't sometimes differ,
What a notable mistake
Providence would have committed!
To adore thee, sweetest Cynthia, [aside
Is the height of all my wishes:
As it well may be, for am I
Worthy, worship even to give her? [Exeunt.

SCENE THE SECOND
A Wood near Rome.

(Enter NISIDA and CHLORIS, the latter with a lyre).

NISIDA.
Have you brought the instrument?

CHLORIS.
Yes.

NISIDA.
     Then give it me, for here

In this tranquil forest sphere,
Where the boughs and blossoms blent,
Ruby blooms and emerald stems,
Round about their radiance fling,
Where the canopy of spring
Breathes of flowers and gleams with gems,
Here I wish that air to play,
Which to words that Cynthia wrote
I have set--a simple note.

CHLORIS.
And the song, senora, say,
What 's the theme?

NISIDA.
    A touching strain,--
How a nightingale in a grove
Singing sweetly of his love,
Sang its pleasure and its pain.

Enter CYNTHIA (reading in a book).

CYNTHIA (to herself).
Whilst each alley here discloses
Youthful nymphs, who as they pass
To Diana's shrine, the grass
Turn to beds of fragrant roses,--
Where the interlac`ed bars
Of these woods their beauty dowers
Seem a verdant sky of flowers--
Seem an azure field of stars.
I shall here recline and read
(While they wander through the grove)

Ovid's 'Remedy of Love.'

NISIDA (to Chloris).
Hear the words and air.

CHLORIS.
    Proceed.

NISIDA (singing).
O nightingale, whose sweet exulting strain
Tells of thy triumphs to the listening grove,
Thou fill'st my heart with envy and with pain.
But no; but no; for if thou sing'st of love,
Jealousy's pangs and sorrow's tears remain.

CYNTHIA (advancing).
What a charming air! To me
What an honour! From this day
I may well be vain, as they
May without presumption be,
Who, despite their numerous slips,
Find their words can please the ear,
Who their rugged verses hear
Turn to music on thy lips.

NISIDA.
'T is thine own genius, not my skill,
That produces this effect;
For, without it, I suspect,
Would my voice sound harsh and shrill,
And my lute's strings should be broken
With a just and wholesome rigour,
For presuming to disfigure

What thy words so well have spoken.
Whither wert thou wending here?

CYNTHIA.
Through the quiet wood proceeding,
I the poet's book was reading,
When there fell upon my ear,
Soft and sweet, thy voice: its power,
Gentle lodestone of my feet,
Brought me to this green retreat--
Led me to this lonely bower:
But what wonder, when to listen
To thy sweetly warbled words
Ceased the music of the birds--
Of the founts that glide and glisten?
May I hope that, since I came
Thus so opportunely near,
I the gloss may also hear?

NISIDA.
I will sing it, though with shame.

(Sings)
Sweet nightingale, that from some echoing grot
Singest the rapture of thy love aloud,
Singest with voice so joyous and so proud,
All unforgetting thou mayst be forgot,
Full of thyself and of thy happy lot!
Ah! when thou trillest that triumphant strain
To all the listening lyrists of the grove,
Thou fill'st my heart with envy and with pain!
But no; but no; for if thou sing'st of love.
Jealousy's pangs and sorrow's tears remain!

Enter DARIA.

DARIA.
Ah! my Nisida, forbear,
Ah! those words forbear to sing,
Which on zephyr's wanton wing
Thou shouldst waft not on the air.
All is wrong, how sweet it be,
That the vestal's thoughts reprove:
What is jealousy? what is love?
That they should be sung by thee?
Think this wood is consecrated
To Diana's service solely,
Not to Venus: it is holy.
Why then wouldst thou desecrate it
With thy songs? Does 't not amaze
Thee thyself--this strangest thing--
In Diana's grove to sing
Hymns of love to Cupid's praise?
But I need not wonder, no,
That thou 'rt so amused, since I
Here see Cynthia with thee.

CYNTHIA.
    Why
Dost thou say so?

DARIA.
    I say so
For good cause: in books profane
Thou unceasingly delightest,
Verse thou readest, verse thou writest,

Of their very vanity vain.
And if thou wouldst have me prove
What I say to thy proceeding,
Tell me, what 's this book thou 'rt reading?

CYNTHIA.
'T is The Remedy of Love.
Whence thou mayst perceive how weak
Is thy inference, thy deduction
From my studious self-instruction;
Since the patient who doth seek
Remedies to cure his pain
Shows by this he would grow better;--
For the slave who breaks his fetter
Cannot surely love his chain.

NISIDA.
This, though not put quite so strong,
Was involved in the conclusion
Of my lay: Love's disillusion
Was the burden of my song.

DARIA.
Remedies and disillusions,
Seek ye both beneath one star?
Ah! if so, you are not far
From its pains and its confusions:
For the very fact of pleading
Disillusion, shows that thou
'Neath illusion's yoke doth bow,--
And the patient who is needing
Remedies doth prove that still
The sharp pang he doth endure,

For there 's no one seeks a cure
Ere he feels that he is ill:--
Therefore to this wrong proceeding
Grieved am I to see ye clinging--
Seeking thou thy cure in singing--
Thou thy remedy in reading.

CYNTHIA.
Casual actions of this class
That are done without intention
Of a second end, to mention
Here were out of place: I pass
To another point: There 's no one
Who with genius, or denied it,--
Dowered with mind, but has applied it
Some especial track to go on:
This variety suffices
For its exercise and action,
Just as some by free attraction
Seek the virtues and the vices;--
This blind instinct, or this duty,
We three share;--'t is thy delight
Nisida to sing,--to write
Mine,--and thine to adore thy beauty.
Which of these three occupations
Is the best--or those that need
Skill and labour to succeed,
Or thine own vain contemplations?--
Have I not, when morning's rays
Gladdened grove and vale and mountain,
Seen thee in the crystal fountain
At thyself enamoured gaze?
Wherefore, once again returning

To our argument of love,
Thou a greater pang must prove,
If from thy insatiate yearning
I infer a cause: the spell
Lighter falls on one who still,
To herself not feeling ill,
Would in other eyes seem well.

DARIA.
Ah! so far, so far from me
Is the wish as vain as weak--
(Now my virtue doth not speak,
Now but speaks my vanity),
Ah! so far, I say, my breast
Turns away from things of love,
That the sovereign hand of Jove,
Were it to attempt its best,
Could no greater wonder work,
Than that I, Daria, should
So be changed in mind and mood
As to let within me lurk
Love's minutest, smallest seed:--
Only upon one condition
Could I love, and that fruition
Then would be my pride indeed.

CYNTHIA.
What may that condition be?

DARIA.
When of all mankind, I knew
One who felt a love so true
As to give his life for me,

Then, until my own life fled,
Him, with gratitude and pride,
Were I sure that so he died,
I would love though he were dead.

NISIDA.
Poor reward for love so great
Were that tardy recollection,
Since, it seems, for thy affection
He, till life is o'er, must wait.

CYNTHIA.
Soars thy vanity so high?
Thy presumption is above
All belief: be sure, for love
No man will be found to die.

DARIA.
Why more words then? love must be
In my case denied by heaven:
Since my love cannot be given
Save to one who 'll die for me.

CYNTHIA.
Thy ambition is a thing
So sublime, what can be said?--
Better I resumed and read,
Better, Nisida, thou shouldst sing,
This disdain so strange and strong,
This delusion little heeding.

NISIDA.
Yes, do thou resume thy reading,

I too will resume my song.

DARIA.
I, that I may not renew
Such reproaches, whilst you sing,
Whilst you read, in this clear spring
Thoughtfully myself shall view.

NISIDA sings.
O nightingale, whose sweet exulting strain
Tells of thy triumphs to the listening grove,
Thou fill'st my heart with envy and with pain!--
But no, but no, for if thou sing'st of love
Jealousy's pangs and sorrow's tears remain!

Enter CHRYSANTHUS, CLAUDIUS, and ESCARPIN.

CLAUDIUS, to Chrysanthus.
Does not the beauty of this wood,
This tranquil wood, delight thee?

CHRYSANTHUS.
    Yes:
Here nature's lord doth dower and bless
The world in most indulgent mood.
Who could believe this greenwood here
For the first time has blessed mine eyes?

CLAUDIUS.
It is the second Paradise,
Of deities the verdant sphere.

CHRYSANTHUS.

'T is more, this green and grassy glade
Whither our careless steps have strolled,
For here three objects we behold
Equally fair by distance made.
Of these that chain our willing feet,
There yonder where the path is leading,
One is a lady calmly reading,
One is a lady singing sweet,
And one whose rapt though idle air
Gives us to understand this truth--
A woman blessed with charms and youth,
Does quite enough in being fair.

ESCARPIN.
You are quite right in that, I 've seen
Beauties enough of that sort too.

CLAUDIUS.
If of the three here given to view,
The choice were thine to choose between,
Which of them best would suit thy taste?
Which wouldst thou make thy choice of, say?

CHRYSANTHUS.
I do not know: for in one way
They so with equal gifts are graced,
So musical and fair and wise,
That while one captivates the mind,
One works her witcheries with the wind,
And one, the fairest, charms our eyes.
The one who sings, it seems a duty,
Trusting her sweet voice, to think sweet,
The one who reads, to deem discreet,

The third, we judge but by her beauty:
And so I fear by act or word
To wrong the three by judging ill,
Of one her charms, of one her skill,
And the intelligence of the third.
For to choose one does wrong to two,
But if I so presumed to dare . . .

CLAUDIUS.
Which would it be?

CHRYSANTHUS.
    The one that 's fair.

ESCARPIN.
My blessings on your choice and you!
That 's my opinion in the case,
'T is plain at least to my discerning
That in a woman wit and learning
Are nothing to a pretty face.

NISIDA.
Chloris, quick, take up the lyre,
For a rustling noise I hear
In this shady thicket near:
Yes, I 'm right, I must retire.
Swift as feet can fly I 'll go.
For these men that here have strayed
Must have heard me while I played. [Exeunt Nisida and Chloris.

CYNTHIA.
One of them I think I know.
Yes, 't is Claudius, as I thought,

Now he has a chance: I 'll see
If he cares to follow me,
Guessing rightly what has brought
Me to-day unto the grove:--
Ah! if love to grief is leading
Of what use to me is reading
In the Remedies of Love? [Exit.

DARIA (to herself).
In these bowers by trees o'ergrown,
Here contented I remain,
All companionship is vain,
Save my own sweet thoughts alone:--

CLAUDIUS.
Dear Chrysanthus, your election
Was to me both loss and gain,
Gave me pleasure, gave me pain:--
It seemed plain to my affection
(Being in love) your choice should fall
On the maid of pensive look,
Not on her who read the book:
But your praise made up for all.
And since each has equal force,
My complaint and gratulation,
Whilst with trembling expectation
I pursue my own love's course,
Try your fortune too, till we
Meet again. [Exit.

CHRYSANTHUS.
    Confused I stay,
Without power to go away,

Spirit-bound, my feet not free.
From the instant that on me,
As a sudden beam might dart,
Flashed that form which Phidian art
Could not reach, I 've known no rest.--
Babylon is in my breast--
Troy is burning in my heart.

ESCARPIN.
Strange that I should feel as you,
That one thought should fire us two,
I too, sir, have lost my senses
Since I saw that lady.

CHRYSANTHUS.
    Who,
Madman! fool! do you speak of? you!
Dare to feel those griefs of mine!--

ESCARPIN.
No, sir, yours I quite resign,
Would I could my own ones too!--

CHRYSANTHUS.
Leave me, or my wrath you 'll rue;
Hence! buffoon: by heaven I swear it,
I will kill you else.

ESCARPIN.
    I go:--
For if you address her, oh!
Could my jealous bosom bear it? [aside [Exit.

CHRYSANTHUS (to Daria).
If my boldness so may dare it,
I desire to ask, senora,
If thou art this heaven's Aurora,
If the goddess of this fountain,
If the Juno of this mountain,
If of these bright flowers the Flora,
So that I may rightly know
In what style should speak to thee
My hushed voice . . . but pardon me
Now I would not thou said'st so.
Looking at thee now, the glow
Of thy beauty so excelleth,
Every charm so plainly telleth
Thou Diana's self must be;
Yes, Diana's self is she,
Who within her grove here dwelleth.

DARIA.
If, before you spoke to me,
You desired my name to know,
I in your case act not so,
Since I speak, whoe'er you be,
Forced, but most unwillingly
(As to listening heaven is plain)
To reply:--a bootless task
Were it in me, indeed, to ask,
Since, whoe'er you be, my strain
Must be one of proud disdain.
So I pray you, cavalier,
Leave me in this lonely wood,
Leave me in the solitude
I enjoyed ere you came here.

CHRYSANTHUS.
Sweetly, but with tone severe,
Thus my error you reprove--
That of asking in this grove
What your name is: you 're so fair,
That, whatever name you bear,
I must tell you of my love.

DARIA.
Love! a word to me unknown,
Sounds so strangely in my ears,
That my heart nor feels nor hears
Aught of it when it has flown.

CHRYSANTHUS.
Then there is no rashness shown
In repeating it once more,
Since to hear or to ignore
Suits alike your stoic coldness.

DARIA.
Yes, the speech, but not the boldness
Of the speaker I pass o'er,
For this word, whate'er it be,
When it breaks upon my ear,
Quick 't is gone, although I hear.

CHRYSANTHUS.
You forget it?

DARIA.
     Instantly.

CHRYSANTHUS.
What! love's sweetest word! ah, me!
Canst forget the mightiest ray
Death can dart, or heaven display?

DARIA.
Yes, for lightning, entering where
Naught resists, is lost in air.

CHRYSANTHUS.
How? what way?

DARIA.
     Well, in this way:
If two doors in one straight line
Open lie, and lightning falls,
Then the bolt between the walls
Passes through, and leaves no sign.
So 't is with this word of thine;
Though love be, which I do n't doubt,
Like heaven's bolt that darts about,
Still two opposite doors I 've here,
And what enters by one ear
By the other ear goes out.

CHRYSANTHUS.
If this lightning then darts through
Where no door lies open wide
To let it pass at the other side,
Must not fire and flame ensue?
This being so, 't is also true
That the fire of love that flies

Into my heart, in flames must rise,
Since without its feast of fire
The fatal flash cannot retire,
That has entered by the eyes.

DARIA.
If to what I said but now
You had listened, I believe
You would have preferred to leave
Still unspoken love's vain vow.
This you would yourself allow.

CHRYSANTHUS.
What then was it?

DARIA.
     I do n't know:
Something 't was that typified
My presumption and my pride.

CHRYSANTHUS.
Let me know it even so.

DARIA.
That in me no love could grow
Save for one who first would die
For my love.

CHRYSANTHUS.
     And death being past,
Would he win your love at last?--

DARIA.

Yes, on that he might rely.

CHRYSANTHUS.
Then I plight my troth that I
Will to that reward aspire,--
A poor offering at the fire
By those beauteous eyes supplied.

DARIA.
But as you have not yet died,
Pray do n't follow me, but retire. [Exit.

CHRYSANTHUS.
In what bosom, at one moment,
Oh! ye heavens! e'er met together[6]
Such a host of anxious troubles?
Such a crowd of boding terrors?
Can I be the same calm student
Who awhile ago here wended?
To a miracle of beauty,
To a fair face now surrendered,
I scarce know what brought me hither,
I my purpose scarce remember.
What bewitchment, what enchantment,
What strange lethargy, what frenzy
Can have to my heart, those eyes
Such divine delirium sent me?
What divinity, desirous
That I should not know the endless
Mysteries of the book I carry,
In my path such snares presenteth,
Seeking from these serious studies
To distract me and divert me?

But what 's this I say? One passion
Accidentally developed,
Should not be enough, no, no,
From myself myself to sever.
If the violence of one star
Draws me to a deity's service,
It compels not; for the planets
Draw, but force not, the affections.
Free is yet my will, my mind too,
Free is still my heart: then let me
Try to solve more noble problems
Than the doubts that love presenteth.
And since Claudius, the new Clytie[7]
Of the sun, whose golden tresses
Lead him in pursuit, her footsteps
Follows through the wood, my servant
Having happily too departed,
And since yonder rocks where endeth
The dark wood in savage wildness
Must be the rude rustic shelter
Of the Christians who fled thither,
I 'll approach them to endeavour
To find there Carpophorus:--
He alone, the wise, the learn`ed,
Can my understanding rescue
From its night-mare dreams and guesses. [Exit.

SCENE III. The extremity of the wood:
wild rocks with the entrance to a cave.
Carpophorus comes forth from the cave, but is for a while unseen by
Chrysanthus, who enters.

CHRYSANTHUS.
What a labyrinthine thicket
Is this place that I have entered!
Nature here takes little trouble,
Letting it be seen how perfect
Is the beauty that arises
Even from nature's careless efforts:
Deep within this darksome grotto
Which no sunbeam's light can enter,
I shall penetrate: it seemeth
As if until now it never
Had been trod by human footsteps.
There where yonder marge impendeth
O'er a streamlet that swift-flying
Carries with it the white freshness
Of the snows that from the mountains
Ever in its waves are melted,
Stands almost a skeleton;
The sole difference it presenteth
To the tree-trunks near it is,
That it moves as well as trembles,
Slow and gaunt, a living corse.
Oh! thou venerable elder
Who, a reason-gifted tree,
Mid mere natural trees here dwelleth.--

CARPOPHORUS.
Wo! oh! wo is me!--a Roman!
(At seeing Chrysanthus, he attempts to fly.)

CHRYSANTHUS.

Though a Roman, do not dread me:
With no evil end I seek thee.

CARPOPHORUS.
Then what wouldst thou have, thou gentle
Roman youth? for thou hast silenced
My first fears even by thy presence.

CHRYSANTHUS.
'T is to ask, what now I ask thee,
Of the rocks that in this desert
Gape for ever open wide
In eternal yawns incessant,
Which is the rough marble tomb
Of a living corse interred here?
Which of these dark caves is that
In whose gloom Carpophorus dwelleth?
'T is important I speak with him.

CARPOPHORUS.
Then, regarding not the perils,
I will own it. I myself
Am Carpophorus.

CHRYSANTHUS.
    Oh! let me,
Father, feel thy arms enfold me.

CARPOPHORUS.
To my heart: for as I press thee,
How, I know not, the mere contact
Brings me back again the freshness
And the greenness of my youth,

Like the vine's embracing tendrils
Twining round an aged tree:
Gallant youth, who art thou? tell me.

CHRYSANTHUS.
Father, I am called Chrysanthus,
Of Polemius, the first member
Of the Roman senate, son.

CARPOPHORUS.
And thy purpose?

CHRYSANTHUS.
    It distresses
Me to see thee standing thus:
On this bank sit down and rest thee.

CARPOPHORUS.
Kindly thought of; for, alas!
I a tottering wall resemble:
At the mouth of this my cave
Let us then sit down together. [*They sit down.*
What now wouldst thou have, Sir Stranger?

CHRYSANTHUS.
Sir, as long as I remember,
I have felt an inclination
To the love of books and letters.
In my casual studies lately
I a difficulty met with
That I could not solve, and knowing
No one in all Rome more learn`ed
Than thyself (thy reputation

Having with this truth impressed me)
I have hither come to ask thee
To explain to me this sentence:
For I cannot understand it.
'T is, sir, in this book.

CARPOPHORUS.
     Pray, let me
See it then.

CHRYSANTHUS.
     'T is at the beginning;
Nay, the sentence that perplexes
Me so much is that.

CARPOPHORUS.
     Why, these
Are the Holy Gospels! Heavens!

CHRYSANTHUS.
What! you kiss the book?

CARPOPHORUS.
     And press it
To my forehead, thus suggesting
The profound respect with which
I even touch so great a treasure.

CHRYSANTHUS.
Why, what is the book, which I
By mere accident selected?

CARPOPHORUS.

'T is the basis, the foundation
Of the Scripture Law.

CHRYSANTHUS.
    I tremble
With an unknown horror.

CARPOPHORUS.
    Why?

CHRYSANTHUS.
Deeper now I would not enter
Into the secrets of a book
Which are magic spells, I 'm certain.

CARPOPHORUS.
No, not so, but vital truths.

CHRYSANTHUS.
How can that be, when its verses
Open with this line that says
(A beginning surely senseless)
"In the beginning was the Word,
And it was with God": and then it
Adds: this Word itself was God;
Then unto the Word reverting,
Says explicitly that IT
"Was made flesh"?

CARPOPHORUS.
    A truth most certain:
For this first evangelist
Here to us our God presenteth

In a twofold way: the first
As being God, as Man the second.

CHRYSANTHUS.
God and Man combined together?

CARPOPHORUS.
Yes, in one eternal Person
Are both natures joined together.

CHRYSANTHUS.
Then, for this is what more presses
On my mind, can that same Word
When it was made flesh, be reckoned
God?

CARPOPHORUS.
    Yes, God and Man is Christ
Crucified for our transgressions.

CHRYSANTHUS.
Pray explain this wondrous problem.

CARPOPHORUS.
He is God, because He never
Was created: He is the Word,
For, besides, He was engendered
By the Father, from both whom
In eternal due procession
Comes the Holy Ghost, three Persons,
But one God, thrice mystic emblem!--
In the Catholic faith we hold
In one Trinity one God dwelleth,

And that in one God is also
One sole Trinity, ever bless`ed,
Which confounds not the three Persons,
Nor the single substance severs.
One is the person of the Father,
One the Son's, beloved for ever,
One, the third, the Holy Ghost's.
But though three, you must remember
That in the Father, and in the Son,
And in the Holy Ghost . . .

CHRYSANTHUS.
    Unheard of
Mysteries these!

CARPOPHORUS.
    There 's but one God,
Equal in the power exerted,
Equal in the state and glory;
For . . .

CHRYSANTHUS.
    I listen, but I tremble.

CARPOPHORUS.
The eternal Father is
Limitless, even so unmeasured
And eternal is the Son,
And unmeasured and eternal
Is the Holy Ghost; but then
Three eternities are not meant here,
Three immensities, no, but One,
Who is limitless and eternal.

For though increate the three,
They are but one Uncreated.
First the Father was not made,
Or created, or engendered;
Then engendered was the Son
By the Father, not created;
And the Spirit was not made
Or created, or engendered
By the Father or the Son,
But proceeds from both together.
This is God's divinity
Viewed as God alone, let 's enter
On the human aspect.

CHRYSANTHUS.
    Stay:
For so strange, so unexpected
Are the things you say, that I
Need for their due thought some leisure.
Let me my lost breath regain,
For entranced, aroused, suspended,
Spell-bound your strong reasons hold me.
Is there then but one sole God
In three Persons, one in essence,
One in substance, one in power,
One in will?

CARPOPHORUS.
    My son, 't is certain.

(Enter Aurelius and Soldiers.)

AURELIUS to the Soldiers.

Yonder is the secret cavern
Of Carpophorus, at its entrance
See him seated with another
Reading.

A SOLDIER.
     Why delay? Arrest them.

AURELIUS.
Recollect Polemius bade us,
When we seized them, to envelope
Each one's face, that so, the Christians,
Their accomplices and fellows,
Should not know or recognize them.

A SOLDIER.
You 're our prisoners.
[A veil is thrown over the head of each.]

CHRYSANTHUS.
     What! base wretches . . .

AURELIUS.
Gag their mouths.

CHRYSANTHUS.
     But then I am . . .

AURELIUS.
Come, no words: now tie together
Both their hands behind their backs.

CHRYSANTHUS.

Why I am . . .

CARPOPHORUS.
     Oh! sacred heaven!
Now my wished-for day has come.

A VOICE FROM HEAVEN.
No, not yet, my faithful servant:--
I desire the constancy
Of Chrysanthus may be tested:--
Heed not him, as for thyself,
In this manner I preserve thee. [Carpophorus disappears.

(Enter Polemius.)

POLEMIUS.
What has happened?

AURELIUS.
     Oh! a wonder.--
We Carpophorus arrested,
And with him this other Christian;
Both we held here bound and fettered,
When from out our hands he vanished.

POLEMIUS.
By some sorcery 't was effected,
For those Christians use enchantments,
And then miracles pretend them.

A SOLDIER.
See, a crowd of them there flying
To the mountains.

POLEMIUS.
> Intercept them,
And secure the rabble rout;
This one I shall guard myself here:-- [Exeunt Aurelius and soldiers.
Miserable wretch! who art thou?
Thus that I may know thee better,
Judging from thy face thy crimes,
I unveil thee. Gracious heaven!
My own son!

CHRYSANTHUS.
> Oh! heavens! my father!

POLEMIUS.
Thou with Christians here detected?
Thou here in their caverns hidden?
Thou a prisoner? Wherefore, wherefore,
O immense and mighty Jove,
Are thy angry bolts suspended?

CHRYSANTHUS.
'T was to solve a certain doubt
Which some books of thine presented,
That I sought Carpophorus,
That I wandered to these deserts,
And . . .

POLEMIUS.
> Cease, cease; for now I see
What has led to this adventure:
Thou unhappily art gifted
With a genius ill-directed;

For I count as vain and foolish
All the lore that lettered leisure
Has in human books e'er written;
But this passion has possessed thee,
And to learn their magic rites
Here, a willing slave, has led thee.

CHRYSANTHUS.
No, not magic was the knowledge
I came here to learn--far better--
The high mysteries of a faith
Which I reverence, while I dread them.

POLEMIUS.
Cease, oh! cease once more, nor let
Such vile treason find expression
On thy lips. What! thou to praise them!

AURELIUS (within).
Yonder wait the two together.

POLEMIUS.
Cover up thy face once more,
That the soldiers, when they enter,
May not know thee, may not know
How my honour is affected
By this act, until I try
Means more powerful to preserve it.

CHRYSANTHUS (aside).
God, whom until now I knew not,
Grant Thy favour, deign to help me:
Grant through suffering and through sorrow

I may come to know Thee better.

(Enter Aurelius and Soldiers.)

AURELIUS.
Though we searched the whole of the mountain,
Not one more have we arrested.

POLEMIUS.
Take this prisoner here to Rome,
And be sure that you remember
All of you my strict commands,
That no hand shall dare divest him
Of his veil:-- [Chrysanthus is led out.
    Why, why, O heavens! [aside.
Do I pause, but from my breast here
Tear my bleeding heart? How act
In so dreadful a dilemma?
If I say who he is, I tarnish
With his guilt my name for ever,
And my loyalty if I 'm silent,
Since he being here transgresses
By that fact alone the edict:
Shall I punish him? The offender
Is my son. Shall I free him? He
Is my enemy and a rebel:--
If between these two extremes
Some mean lies, I cannot guess it.
As a father I must love him,
And as a judge I must condemn him. [Exeunt.

ACT THE SECOND.

SCENE I.
A hall in the house of Polemius.

Enter Claudius and Escarpin.

CLAUDIUS.
Has he not returned? Can no one
Guess in the remotest manner[8]
Where he is?

ESCARPIN.
      Sir, since the day
That you left me with my master
In Diana's grove, and I
Had with that divinest charmer
To leave him, no eye has seen him.
Love alone knows how it mads me.

CLAUDIUS.
Of your loyalty I doubt not.

ESCARPIN.
Loyalty 's a different matter,
'T is not wholly that.

CLAUDIUS.
      What then?

ESCARPIN.
Dark suspicions, dismal fancies,
That perhaps to live with her
He lies hid within those gardens.

CLAUDIUS.
If I could imagine that,
I, Escarpin, would be gladdened
Rather than depressed.

ESCARPIN.
    I 'm not:--
I am filled, like a full barrel,
With depressions.

CLAUDIUS.
    And for what?

ESCARPIN.
Certain wild chimeras haunt me,
Jealousy doth tear my heart,
And despairing love distracts me.

CLAUDIUS.
You in love and jealous?

ESCARPIN.
    I
Jealous and in love. Why marvel?
Am I such a monster?

CLAUDIUS.

               What!
With Daria?

ESCARPIN.
          'T is no matter
What her name is, or Daria
Or Maria, I would have her
Both subjective and subjunctive,
She verb passive, I verb active.

CLAUDIUS.
You to love so rare a beauty?

ESCARPIN.
Yes, her beauty, though uncommon,
Would lack something, if it had not
My devotion.

CLAUDIUS.
          How? explain:--

ESCARPIN.
Well, I prove it in this manner:--
Mr. Dullard fell in love
(I do n't tell where all this happened,
Or the time, for of the Dullards
Every age and time give samples)
With a very lovely lady:
At her coach-door as he chattered
One fine evening, he such nonsense
Talked, that one who heard his clatter,
Asked the lady in amazement
If this simpleton's advances

Did not make her doubt her beauty?--
But she quite gallantly answered,
Never until now have I
Felt so proud of my attractions,
For no beauty can be perfect
That all sorts of men do n't flatter.

CLAUDIUS.
What a feeble jest!

ESCARPIN.
      This feeble?--

CLAUDIUS.
Yes, the very type of flatness:--
Cease buffooning, for my uncle
Here is coming.

ESCARPIN.
     Of his sadness
Plainly is his face the mirror.

Enter Polemius and servants.

CLAUDIUS.
Jupiter doth know the anguish,
My good lord, with which I venture
To approach thee since this happened.

POLEMIUS.
Claudius, as thine own, I 'm sure,
Thou dost feel this great disaster.

The Two Lovers of Heaven: Chrysanthus and Daria

CLAUDIUS.
I my promise gave thee that
To Chrysanthus . . .

POLEMIUS.
    Cease; I ask thee
Not to proffer these excuses,
Since I do not care to have them.

CLAUDIUS.
Then it seems that all thy efforts
Have been useless to unravel
The strange mystery of his fate?

POLEMIUS.
With these questions do not rack me;
For, though I would rather not
Give the answer, still the answer
Rises with such ready aptness
To my lips from out my heart,
That I scarcely can withstand it.

CLAUDIUS.
Why conceal it then from me,
Knowing that thy blood meanders
Through my veins, and that my life
Owns thee as its lord and master?--
Oh! my lord, confide in me,
Let thy tongue speak once the language
That thine eyes so oft have spoken.

POLEMIUS.
Let the servants leave the apartment.

ESCARPIN (aside).
Ah! if beautiful Daria
Would but favour my attachment,
Though I have no house to give her,
Lots of stories I can grant her:-- [Exeunt Escarpin and servants.

CLAUDIUS.
Now, my lord, we are alone.

POLEMIUS.
Listen then; for though to baffle
Thy desire were my intention,
By my miseries overmastered,
I am forced to tell my secret;
Not so much have I been granted
License to avow my sufferings,
But I am, as 't were commanded
Thus to break my painful silence,
Doing honestly, though sadly,
Willingly the fact disclosing,
Which by force had been extracted.
Hear it, Claudius: my Chrysanthus,
My Chrysanthus is not absent:
In this very house he 's living!--
Would the gods, ah! me, had rather
Made a tomb and not a prison
Of his present locked apartment!
Which is in this house, within it
Is he prisoned, chained, made captive.
This surprises thee, no wonder:
More surprised thou 'lt be hereafter,
When thou com'st to know the reason

Of a fact so strange and startling.
On that fatal day, when I
Sought the mount and thou the garden,
Him I found where thou didst lose him,
Near the wood where he had rambled:
He was taken by my soldiers
At the entrance of a cavern,
With Carpophorus:--oh! here
Patience, patience may heaven grant me!--
It was lucky that they did not
See his face, for thus it happened
That the front of my dishonour
Was not in his face made patent:
Him they captured without knowing
Who he was, it being commanded
That the faces of the prisoners
Should be covered, but ere captured
This effectually was done
By themselves, they flying backward
With averted faces; he
Thus was taken, but his partner,
That strange prodigy of Rome--
Man in mind, wild beast in manners,
Doubly thus a prodigy--
Saved himself by power of magic.
Thus Chrysanthus was sole prisoner,
While the Christian crowd, disheartened,
Fled for safety to the mountains
From their grottoes and their caverns.
These the soldiers quickly followed,
And behind in that abandoned
Savage place remained but two--
Two, oh! think, a son and father.--

One a judge, too, in a cause
Wicked, bad, beyond example,
In a cause that outraged Caesar,
And the gods themselves disparaged.
There with a delinquent son
Stood I, therefore this should happen,
That both clemency and rigour
In my heart waged fearful battle--
Clemency in fine had won,
I would have removed the bandage
From his eyes and let him fly,
But that instant, ah! unhappy!
Came the soldiers back, and then
It were but more misery added,
If they knew of my connivance:
All that then my care could manage
To protect him was the secret
Of his name to keep well guarded.
Thus to Rome I brought him prisoner,
Where pretending great exactness,
That his friends should not discover
Where this Christian malefactor
Was imprisoned, to this house,
To my own house, I commanded
That he should be brought; there hidden
And unknown, a few days after
I in his place substituted . . .
Ah! what will not the untrammelled
Strength of arbitrary power
Dare attempt? what law not trample?
Substituted, I repeat,
For my son a slave, whose strangled,
Headless corse thus paid the debt

Which from me were else exacted.
You will say, "Since fortune thus
Has the debt so happily cancelled,
Why imprison or conceal him?"--
And, thus, full of doubts, I answer
That though it is true I wished not,
Woe is me! the common scaffold
Should his punishment make public,
I as little wished his hardened
Heart should know my love and pity
Since it did not fear my anger:
Ah! believe me, Claudius,
'Twixt the chastisement a father
And an executioner gives,
A great difference must be granted:
One hand honours what it striketh,
One disgraces, blights, and blackens.
Soon my rigour ceased, for truly,
In a father's heart it lasteth
Seldom long: but then what wonder,
If the hand that in its anger
Smites his son, in his own breast
Leaves a wound that ever rankles--
I one day his prison entered
With the wish (I own it frankly)
To forgive him, and when I
Thought he would have even thanked me
For receiving a reproof,
Not severe, too lenient rather,
He began to praise the Christians
With such earnestness and ardour,
In defence of their new law,
That my clemency departed,

And my angrier mood returned.
I his doors and windows fastened.
In the room where he is lying,
Well secured by gyves and shackles,
Sparingly his food is given him,
Through my hands alone it passes,
For I dare not to another
Trust the care his state demandeth.
You will think in this I reached to
The extreme of my disasters--
The full limits of misfortune,
But not so, and if you hearken,
You 'll perceive they 're but beginning,
And not ended, as you fancied.
All these strange events so much
Have unnerved him and unmanned him,
That, forgetful of himself,
Of himself he is regardless.
Nothing to the purpose speaks he.
In his incoherent language
Frenzy shows itself, delusion
In his thoughts and in his fancies:--
Many times I 've listened to him,
Since so high-strung and abstracted
Is his mind, he takes no note of
Who goes in or who departeth.
Once I heard him deprecating
Some despotic beauty's hardness,
Saying, "Since I die for thee,
Thou thy favour sure wilt grant me".
At another time he said,
"Three in one, oh! how can that be?"
Things which these same Christian people

In their law hold quite established.
Thus it is my life is troubled,
Lost in doubts, emeshed, and tangled.
If to freedom I restore him,
I have little doubt that, darkened
By the Christian treachery, he
Will declare himself instanter
Openly a Christian, which
Would to me be such a scandal,
That my blood henceforth were tainted,
And my noble name were branded.
If I leave him here in prison,
So excessive is his sadness,
So extreme his melancholy,
That I fear 't will end in madness.
In a word, I hold, my nephew,
Hold it as a certain axiom,
That these dark magician Christians
Keep him bound by their enchantments;
Who through hatred of my house,
And my office to disparage,
Now revenge themselves on me
Through my only son Chrysanthus.
Tell me, then, what shall I do;
But before you give the answer
Which your subtle wit may dictate,
I would with your own eyes have thee
See him first, you 'll then know better
What my urgent need demandeth.
Come, he 's not far off, his quarter
Is adjoining this apartment;
When you see him, I am certain
You will think it a disaster

Far less evil he should die,
Than that in this cruel manner
He should outrage his own blood,
And my bright escutcheon blacken.
[He opens a door, and Chrysanthus is seen seated in a chair, with his hands and feet in irons.]

CLAUDIUS.
Thus to see my friend, o'erwhelms me
With a grief I cannot master.

POLEMIUS.
Stay, do not approach him nearer;
For I would not he remarked thee,
I would save him the disgrace
Of being seen by thee thus shackled.

CLAUDIUS.
What his misery may dictate
We can hear, nor yet attract him.

CHRYSANTHUS.
Was ever human fate so strange as mine?
  Were unmatched wishes ever mated so?
  Is it not enough to feel one form of woe,
Without being forced 'neath opposite forms to pine?
A triune God's mysterious power divine,
  From heaven I ask for life, that I may know,
  From heaven I ask for death, life's grisly foe,
A fair one's favour in my heart to shrine:
But how can death and life so well agree,
  That I can ask of heaven to end their strife,
And grant them both in pitying love to me?

Yet I will ask, though both with risks are rife,
Neither shall hinder me, for heaven must be
  The arbiter of death as well as life.

POLEMIUS.
See now if I spoke the truth.

CLAUDIUS.
I am utterly distracted. (The door closes.

POLEMIUS.
Lest perhaps he should perceive us,
Let us move a little further.
Now advise me how to act,
Since you see the grief that racks me.

CLAUDIUS.
Though it savours of presumption
To white hairs like yours, to hazard
Words of council, yet at times
Even a young man may impart them:
Well-proportioned punishment
Grave defects oft counteracteth.
But when carried to extremes,
It but irritates and hardens.
Any instrument of music
Of this truth is an example.
Lightly touched, it breathes but sweetness,
Discord, when 't is roughly handled.
'T is not well to send an arrow
To such heights, that in discharging
The strong tension breaks the bowstring,
Or the bow itself is fractured.

These two simple illustrations
Are sufficiently adapted
To my purpose, of advising
Means of cure both mild and ample.
You must take a middle course,
All extremes must be abandoned.
Gentle but judicious treatment
Is the method for Chrysanthus.
For severer methods end in
Disappointment and disaster.
Take him, then, from out his prison,
Leave him free, unchecked, untrammelled,
For the danger is an infant
Without strength to hurt or harm him.
Be it that those wretched Christians
Have bewitched him, disenchant him,
Since you have the power; for Nature
With such careful forethought acteth,
That an antidotal herb
She for every poison planteth.
And if, finally, your wish
Is that he this fatal sadness
Should forget, and wholly change it
To a happier state and gladder,
Get him married: for remember
Nothing is so well adapted
To restrain discursive fancies
As the care and the attachment
Centered in a wife and children;
Taking care that in this matter
Mere convenience should not weigh
More than his own taste and fancy:
Let him choose his wife himself.

Pleased in that, to rove or ramble
Then will be beyond his power,
Even were he so attracted,
For a happy married lover
Thinks of naught except his rapture.

POLEMIUS.
I with nothing such good counsel
Can repay, except the frankness
Of accepting it, which is
The reward yourself would ask for.
And since I a mean must choose
Between two extremes of action,
From his cell, to-day, my son
Shall go forth, but in a manner
That will leave his seeming freedom
Circumscribed and safely guarded.
Let that hall which looketh over
Great Apollo's beauteous garden
Be made gay by flowing curtains,
Be festooned by flowery garlands;
Costly robes for him get ready;
Then invite the loveliest damsels
Rome can boast of, to come hither
To the feasts and to the dances.
Bring musicians, and in fine
Let it be proclaimed that any
Woman of illustrious blood
Who from his delusive passions
Can divert him, by her charms
Curing him of all his sadness,
Shall become his wife, how humble
Her estate, her wealth how scanty.

And if this be not sufficient,
I will give a golden talent
Yearly to the leech who cures him
By some happy stroke of practice. [Exit.

CLAUDIUS.
Oh! a father's pitying love,
What will it not do, what marvel
Not attempt for a son's welfare,
For his life?

Enter ESCARPIN.

ESCARPIN.
    My lord 'por Baco!'
(That 's the god I like to swear by,
Jolly god of all good rascals)
May I ask you what 's the secret?

CLAUDIUS.
You gain little when you ask me
For a secret all may know.
After his mysterious absence
Your young lord 's returned home ill.

ESCARPIN.
In what way?

CLAUDIUS.
    That none can fathom,
Since he does not tell his ailment
Save by signs and by his manner.

ESCARPIN.
Then he 's wrong, sir, not to tell it
Clearly: with extreme exactness
Should our griefs, our pains be mentioned.
A back tooth a man once maddened,
And a barber came to draw it.
As he sat with jaws expanded,
"Which tooth is it, sir, that pains you?"
Asked of him the honest barber,
And the patient in affected
Language grandly thus made answer,
"The penultimate"; the dentist
Not being used to such pedantic
Talk as this, with ready forceps
Soon the last of all extracted.
The poor patient to be certain,
With his tongue the spot examined,
And exclaimed, his mouth all bleeding,
"Why, that 's not the right tooth, master".
"Is it not the ultimate molar?"
Said the barber quite as grandly.
"Yes" (he answered), "but I said
The penultimate, and I 'd have you
Know, your worship, that it means
Simply that that 's next the farthest".
Thus instructed, he returned
To the attack once more, remarking
"In effect then the bad tooth
Is the one that 's next the last one?"
"Yes", he said, "then here it is",
Spoke the barber with great smartness,
Plucking out the tooth that then
Was the last but one; it happened

From not speaking plain, he lost
Two good teeth, and kept his bad one.

CLAUDIUS.
Come and something newer learn
In the stratagem his father
Has arranged to cure the illness
Of Chrysanthus, whom he fancies . . .

ESCARPIN.
What?

CLAUDIUS.
     Is spell-bound by the Christians
Through the power of their enchantments:--
(Since to-day I cannot see thee, [aside.
Cynthia fair, forgive my absence). [Exit.

ESCARPIN.
While these matters thus proceed,
I shall try, let what will happen,
Thee to see, divine Daria:--
At my love, oh! be not angered,
Since the penalty of beauty
Is to be beloved: then pardon. [Exit.

SCENE II.--The Wood.

Enter DARIA from the chase with bow and arrows.

DARIA.
O stag that swiftly flying
Before my feathered shafts the winds outvieing,
Impelled by wings, not feet,
If in this green retreat
Here panting thou wouldst die,
And stain with blood the fountain murmuring by,
Await another wound, another friend,
That so with quicker speed thy life may end;
For to a wretch that stroke a friend must be
That eases death and sooner sets life free.
[She stumbles and falls near the mouth of a cave.]
But, bless me, heaven! I feel
My brain grow hot, my curdling blood congeal:
A form of fire and snow
I seem at once to turn: this sudden blow,
This stumbling, how I know not, by this stone,
This horrid mouth in which my grave is shown,
This cave of many shapes,
Through which the melancholy mountain gapes,
This mountain's self, a vast
Abysmal shadow cast
Suddenly on my heart, as if 't were meant
To be my rustic pyre, my strange new monument,
All fill my heart with wonder and with fear,
What buried mysteries are hidden here
That terrify me so,
And make me tremble 'neath impending woe.
[A solemn strain of music is heard from within.]
Nay more, illusion now doth bear to me
The sweetest sounds of dulcet harmony,
Music and voice combine:--
O solitude! what phantasms are thine!

But let me listen to the voice that blent
Sounds with the music of the instrument.

Music from within the cave.

SONG.
Oh! be the day for ever blest,
And blest be pitying heaven's decree,
That makes the darksome cave to be
Daria's tomb, her place of rest!

DARIA.
Blest! can such evil auguries bless?
And happy can that strange fate be
That gives this darksome cave to me
As monument of my sad life?

MUSIC.
     Yes.

DARIA.
Oh! who before in actual woe
The happier signs of bliss could read?
Will not a fate so rigorous lead
To misery, not to rapture?--

MUSIC.
     No.

DARIA.
O fantasy! unwelcome guest!
How can this cave bring good to me?

MUSIC.
Itself will tell, when it shall be
Daria's tomb, her place of rest.

DARIA.
But then, who gave the stern decree,
That this dark cave my bones should hide?

MUSIC.
Daria, it was he who died,
Who gave his life for love of thee.

DARIA.
"Who gave his life for love of me!"
Ah! me, and can it be in sooth
That gentle noble Roman youth
I answered with such cruelty
In this same wood the other day,
Saying that I his love would be
If he would only die for me!
Can he have cast himself away
Down this dark cave, and there lies dead,
Buried within the dread abyss,
Waiting my love, his promised bliss?--
My soul, not now mine own, has fled!

CYNTHIA (within).
Forward! forward! through the gloom
Every cave and cavern enter,
Search the dark wood to its centre,
Lest it prove Daria's tomb.

DARIA.

Ah! me, the sense confounding,
Both here and there are opposite voices sounding.
Here is my name in measured cadence greeted,
And there in hollow echoes oft repeated.
Would that the latter cries that reach my ear
Came from my mates in this wild forest sphere,
In the dread solitude that doth surround me
Their presence would be welcome.
[Enter Cynthia with bow and arrows.]

CYNTHIA.
    Till I found me,
Beauteous Daria, by thy side once more,
Each mountain nook my search had well gone o'er.

DARIA (aside).
Let me dissemble
The terror and surprise that make me tremble,
If I have power to feign
Amid the wild confusion of my brain:--
Following the chase to-day,
Wishing Diana's part in full to play,
So fair the horizon smiled,
I left the wood and entered on the wild,
Led by a wounded deer still on and on.
And further in pursuit I would have gone,
Nor had my swift career
Even ended here,
But for this mouth that opening in the rock,
With horrid gape my vain attempt doth mock,
And stops my further way.

CYNTHIA.

Until I found thee I was all dismay,
Lest thou some savage beast, some monstrous foe,
Hadst met.

DARIA (aside).
     Ah! would to Jove 't were so!
And that my death in his wild hands had paid
For future chastisement by fate delayed!
But ah! the wish is vain,
Foreboding horror fills my heart and brain,
This mystic music borne upon the air
Must surely augur ill.

(Enter NISIDA.)

NISIDA.
     Daria fair,
And Cynthia wise, I come to seek ye two.

CYNTHIA.
Has any thing occurred or strange or new?

NISIDA.
I scarce can tell it. As I came along,
I heard a man, in a clear voice and strong,
Proclaiming as he went
Through all the mountain a most strange event:
Rome hath decreed
Priceless rewards to her whose charms may lead
Through lawful love and in an open way
By public wedlock in the light of day,
The son of proud Polemius from the state
Of gloom in which his mind is sunk of late.

CYNTHIA.
And what can be the cause that he is so?

NISIDA.
Ah! that I do not know,
But yonder, leaving the Salarian Way,
A Roman soldier hitherward doth stray:
He may enlighten us and tell us all.

CYNTHIA.
Yes, let us know the truth, the stranger call.

DARIA (aside).
Ah! how distinct the pain
That presses on my heart, and dulls my wildered brain!

(Enter Escarpin.)

NISIDA.
Thou, O thou, whose wandering footsteps
These secluded groves have entered . . .[9]

ESCARPIN.
Thou four hundred times repeated--
Thou and all the thous, your servant.

NISIDA.
Tell us of the proclamation
Publicly to-day presented
To the gaze of Rome.

ESCARPIN.

         I 'll do so;
For there 's nothing I love better
Than a story (aside, if to tell it
In divine Daria's presence
Does not put me out, for no one,
When the loved one listens, ever
Speaks his best): Polemius,
Rome's great senator, whose bended
Shoulders, like an Atlas, bear
All the burden of the empire,
By Numerian's self entrusted,
He, this chief of Rome's great senate,
Has a son, by name Chrysanthus,
Who, as rumour goes, at present
Is afflicted by a sadness
So extreme and so excessive,
That 't is thought to be occasioned
By the magic those detested
Christians (who abhor his house,
And his father, who hath pressed them
Heavily as judge and ruler)
Have against his life effected,
All through hatred of our gods.
And so great is the dejection
That he feels, there 's nothing yet
Found to rouse him or divert him.
Thus it is Numerianus,
Who is ever well-affected
To his father, hath proclaimed
All through Rome, that whosoever
Is so happy by her beauty,
Or so fortunately clever
By her wit, or by her graces

Is so powerful, as to temper
His affliction, since love conquers
All things by his magic presence,
He will give her (if a noble)
As his wife, and will present her
With a portion far surpassing
All Polemius' self possesses,
Not to speak of what is promised
Him whose skill may else effect it.
Thus it is that Rome to-day
Laurel wreaths and crowns presenteth
To its most renowned physicians,
To its sages and its elders,
And to wit and grace and beauty
Joyous feasts and courtly revels;
So that there is not a lady
In all Rome, but thinks it certain
That the prize is hers already,
Since by all 't will be contested,
Some through vanity, and some
Through a view more interested:
Even the ugly ones, I warrant,
Will be there well represented.
So with this, adieu. (Aside, Oh! fairest
Nymph Daria, since I ventured
Here to see thee, having seen thee
Now, alas! I must absent me!) [Exit.

CYNTHIA.
What strange news!

NISIDA.
    There 's not a beauty

But for victory will endeavour
When among Rome's fairest daughters
Such a prize shall be contested.

CYNTHIA.
Thus by showing us the value
Thou upon the victory settest,
We may understand that thou
Meanest in the lists to enter.

NISIDA.
Yes, so far as heaven through music
Its most magic cures effecteth,
Since no witchcraft is so potent
But sweet music may dispel it.
It doth tame the raging wild beast,
Lulls to sleep the poisonous serpent,
And makes evil genii, who
Are revolted spirits--rebels--
Fly in fear, and in this art
I have always been most perfect:
Wrongly would I act to-day,
In not striving for the splendid
Prize which will be mine, when I
See myself the loved and wedded
Wife of the great senator's son,
And the mistress of such treasures.

CYNTHIA.
Although music is an art
Which so many arts excelleth,
Still in truth 't is but a sound
Which the wanton air disperses.

It the sweet child of the air
In the air itself must perish.
I, who in my studious reading
Have such learn`ed lore collected,
Who in poetry, that art
Which both teacheth and diverteth,
May precedence claim o'er many
Geniuses so prized at present,
Can a surer victory hope for
In the great fight that impendeth,
Since the music of the soul
Is what keeps the mind suspended.
In one item, Nisida,
We two differ: thy incentive
Thy chief motive, is but interest:
Mine is vanity, a determined
Will no other woman shall
Triumph o'er me in this effort,
Since I wish that Rome should see
That the glory, the perfection
Of a woman is her mind,
All her other charms excelling.

DARIA.
Interest and vanity
Are the two things, as you tell me,
That, O Cynthia! can oblige thee,
That, O Nisida, can compel thee
To attempt this undertaking
By so many risks attended.
But I think you both are wrong,
Since in this case, having heard that
The affliction this man suffers

Christian sorcery hath effected
Through abhorrence of our gods,
By that atheist sect detested,
Neither of these feelings should
Be your motive to attempt it.
I then, who, for this time only
Will believe these waves that tell me--
These bright fountains--that the beauty
Which so oft they have reflected
Is unequalled, mean to lay it
As an offering in the temple
Of the gods, to show what little
Strength in Christian sorcery dwelleth.

NISIDA.
Then 't is openly admitted
That we three the list will enter
For the prize.

CYNTHIA.
    And from this moment
That the rivalry commences.

NISIDA.
Voice of song, thy sweet enchantment
On this great occasion lend me,
That through thy soft influence
Rank and riches I may merit. [Exit.

CYNTHIA.
Genius, offspring of the soul,
Prove this time thou 'rt so descended,
That thy proud ambitious hopes

May the laurel crown be tendered. [Exit.

DARIA.
Beauty, daughter of the gods,
Now thy glorious birth remember:
Make me victress in the fight,
That the gods may live for ever. [Exit.

SCENE III.--A hall in the house of Polemius, opening at the end upon a garden.

(Enter Polemius and Claudius.)

POLEMIUS.
Is then everything prepared?--

CLAUDIUS.
Everything has been got ready
As you ordered. This apartment
Opening on the garden terrace
Has been draped and covered over
With the costliest silks and velvets,
Leaving certain spaces bare
For the painter's magic pencil,
Where, so cunning is his art,
That it nature's self resembles.
Flowers more fair than in the garden,
Pinks and roses are presented:
But what wonder when the fountains
Still run after to reflect them?--

All things else have been provided,
Music, dances, gala dresses;
And for all that, Rome yet knows not
What in truth is here projected;
'T is a fair Academy,
In whose floral halls assemble
Beauty, wit, and grace, a sight
That we see but very seldom.
All the ladies too of Rome
Have prepared for the contention
With due circumspection, since
As his wife will be selected
She who best doth please him; thus
There are none but will present them
In these gardens, some to see him,
Others to show off themselves here.

POLEMIUS.
Oh, my Claudius, would to Jove
That all this could dispossess me
Of my dark foreboding fancies,
Of the terrors that oppress me!--

(Enter Aurelius.)

AURELIUS.
Sir, a very learned physician
Comes to proffer his best service
To Chrysanthus, led by rumour
Of his illness.

POLEMIUS.
    Bid him enter.

[Aurelius retires, and returns immediately with Carpophorus, disguised as a physician.]

CARPOPHORUS (aside).
Heaven, that I may do the work
That this day I have attempted,
Grant me strength a little while;
For I know my death impendeth!--
Mighty lord, thy victor hand, [aloud.
Let me kiss and kneeling press it.

POLEMIUS.
Venerable elder, rise
From the ground; thy very presence
Gives me joy, a certain instinct
Even at sight of thee doth tell me
Thou alone canst save my son.

CARPOPHORUS.
Heaven but grant the cure be perfect!

POLEMIUS.
Whence, sir, art thou?

CARPOPHORUS.
  Sir, from Athens.

POLEMIUS.
'T is a city that excelleth
All the world in knowledge.

CARPOPHORUS.
  There

All are teachers, all are learners.
The sole wish to be of use
Has on this occasion led me
From my home. Inform me then
How Chrysanthus is affected.

POLEMIUS.
With an overwhelming sadness;
Or to speak it more correctly
(Since when we consult a doctor
Even suspicions should be mentioned),
He, my son, has been bewitched;--
Thus it is these Christian perverts
Take revenge through him on me:
In particular an elder
Called Carpophorus, a wizard . . .
May the day soon come for vengeance!

CARPOPHORUS.
May heaven grant it . . . (aside, For that day
I the martyr's crown may merit).
Where at present is Chrysanthus?

POLEMIUS.
He is just about to enter:--
You can see him; all his ailment
In the soul you 'll find is centered.

CARPOPHORUS.
In the soul then I will cure him,
If my skill heaven only blesses. [Music is heard from within.

CLAUDIUS.

That he 's leaving his apartment
This harmonious strain suggesteth,
Since to counteract his gloom
He by music is attended.
(Enter Chrysanthus richly dressed, preceded by musicians playing and singing, and followed by attendants.)

CHRYSANTHUS.
Cease; my pain, perchance my folly,
Cannot be by song diverted;
Music is a power exerted
For the cure of melancholy,
Which in truth it but augmenteth.

A MUSICIAN.
This your father bade us do.

CHRYSANTHUS.
'T is because he never knew
Pain like that which me tormenteth.
For if he that pang incessant
Felt, he would not wish to cure it,
He would love it and endure it.

POLEMIUS.
Think, my son, that I am present,
And that I am not ambitious
To assume your evil mood,
But to find that it is good.

CHRYSANTHUS.
No, sir, you mistake my wishes.
I would not through you relieve me

Of my care; my former state
Seemed, though, more to mitigate
What I suffer: why not leave me
There to die?

POLEMIUS.
    That yet I may,
Pitying your sad condition,
Work your cure:--A great physician
Comes to visit you to-day.

CHRYSANTHUS (aside).
Who do I behold? ah, me!

CARPOPHORUS.
I will speak to him with your leave.

CHRYSANTHUS (aside).
No, my eyes do not deceive,
'T is Carpophorus that I see!
I my pleasure must conceal.

CARPOPHORUS.
Sir, of what do you complain?

CHRYSANTHUS.
Since you come to cure my pain,
I will tell you how I feel.
A great sadness hath been thrown
O'er my mind and o'er my feelings,
A dark blank whose dim revealings
Make their sombre tints mine own.

CARPOPHORUS.
Can you any cause assign me
Whence this sadness is proceeding?

CHRYSANTHUS.
From my earliest years to reading
Did my studious tastes incline me.
Something thus acquired doth wake
Doubts, and fears, and hopes, ah me!
That the things I read may be.

CARPOPHORUS.
Then from me this lesson take.
Every mystery how obscure,
Is explained by faith alone;
All is clear when that is known:
'T is through faith I 'll work your cure.
Since in that your healing lies,
Take it then from me.

CHRYSANTHUS.
     From you
I infer all good: that true
Faith I hope which you advise.

CARPOPHORUS (to Polemius).
Give me leave, sir, to address
Some few words to him alone,
Less reserve will then be shown. (The two retire to one side.
Have you recognized me?

CHRYSANTHUS.
     Yes,

Every sign shows you are he
Who in my most perilous strait
Fled and left me to my fate.

CARPOPHORUS.
God did that; and would you see
That it was His own work, say,
If I did not then absent me
Through His means, could I present me
As your teacher here to-day?

CHRYSANTHUS.
No.

CARPOPHORUS.
      How just His providence!
Since I was preserved, that I
Here might seek you, and more nigh
Give you full intelligence
Leisurely of every doubt
Which disturbs you when you read.

CHRYSANTHUS.
Mysteries they are indeed,
Difficult to be made out.

CARPOPHORUS.
To the believer all is plain.

CHRYSANTHUS.
I would believe, what must I do?--

CARPOPHORUS.

Your intellectual pride subdue.

CHRYSANTHUS.
I will subdue it, since 't is vain.

CARPOPHORUS.
Then the first thing to be done
Is to be baptized.

CHRYSANTHUS.
    I bow,
Father, and implore it now.

CARPOPHORUS.
Let us for the present shun
Further notice; lest suspicion
Should betray what we would smother;
Every day we 'll see each other,
When I 'll execute my mission:
I, to cure sin's primal scath,
Will at fitting time baptize you,
Taking care to catechise you
In the principles of the faith;
Only now one admonition
Must I give; be armed, be ready
For the fight most fierce and steady
Ever fought for man's perdition;
Oh! take heed, amid the advances
Of the fair who wish to win you,
'Mid the fires that burn within you,
'Mid lascivious looks and glances,
'Mid such various foes enlisted,
That you are not conquered by them.

CHRYSANTHUS.
Women! oh! who dare defy them
By such dread allies assisted?

CARPOPHORUS.
He whom God assists.

CHRYSANTHUS.
    Be swayed
By my tears, and ask him.

CARPOPHORUS.
    You
Must too ask him: for he who
Aids himself, him God doth aid.

POLEMIUS.
What, sir, think you of his case?

CARPOPHORUS.
I have ordered him a bath,
Strong restoring powers it hath,
Which his illness must displace:--

POLEMIUS.
Sir, relying on you then,
I will give you ample wealth,
If you can restore his health.

CARPOPHORUS.
Still I cannot tell you when,
But I shall return and see him

Frequently; in fact 'till he
Is from all his ailment free,
From my hand I will not free him.

POLEMIUS.
For your kindness I am grateful.

CHRYSANTHUS.
He alone has power to cure me.
Since he knows what will allure me,
When all other modes are hateful. [Exit Carpophorus.

(Enter Escarpin.)

ESCARPIN.
All this garden of delight
Must be beauty's birth-place sure,
Here the fresh rose doubly pure,
Here the jasmin doubly white,
Learn to-day a newer grace,
Lovelier red, more dazzling snow.

POLEMIUS.
Why?

ESCARPIN.
     Because the world doth show
Naught so fair as this sweet place.
Falsely boasts th' Elysian bower
Peerless beauty, here to-day
More, far more, these groves display:--
Not a fountain, tree, or flower . . .

POLEMIUS.
Well?

ESCARPIN.
      But by a nymph more fair
Is surpassed.

POLEMIUS.
      Come, Claudius, come,
He will be but dull and dumb,
Shy the proffered bliss to share,
Through the fear and the respect
Which, as son, he owes to me.

CLAUDIUS.
He who gave the advice should see
Also after the effect.
Let us all from this withdraw.

POLEMIUS.
Great results I hope to gather:

ESCARPIN (aside).
Well, you 're the first pander-father
Ever in my life I saw.

CHRYSANTHUS.
What, Escarpin, you, as well,
Going to leave me? Mum for once.

ESCARPIN.
Silence suits me for the nonce.

CHRYSANTHUS.
Why?

ESCARPIN.
      A tale in point I 'll tell:
Once a snuffler, by a pirate
Moor was captured, who in some
Way affected to be dumb,
That his ransom at no high rate
Might be purchased: when his owner
This defect perceived, the shuffle
Made him sell this Mr. Snuffle
Very cheaply: to the donor
Of his freedom, through his nose,
Half in snuffle, half in squeak,
Then he said, "Oh! Moor, I speak,
I 'm not dumb as you suppose".
"Fool, to let your folly lead you
So astray", replied the Moor.
"Had I heard you speak, be sure
I for nothing would have freed you".
Thus it is I moderate me
In the use of tongue and cheek,
Lest when you have heard me speak,
Still more cheaply you may rate me.

CHRYSANTHUS.
You must know the estimation
I have held you in so long.

ESCARPIN.
Well, my memory is not strong.
It requires consideration

To admit that pleasant fact.

CHRYSANTHUS.
What of me do people say?--

ESCARPIN.
Shall I speak it?

CHRYSANTHUS.
    Speak.

ESCARPIN.
    Why, they
Say, my lord, that you are cracked.

CHRYSANTHUS.
For what reason? Why this blame?

ESCARPIN.
Reason, sir, need not be had,
For the wisest man is mad
If he only gets the name.

CHRYSANTHUS.
Well, it was not wrongly given,
If they only knew that I
Have consented even to die
So to reach the wished-for heaven
Of a sovereign beauty's favour.

ESCARPIN.
For a lady's favour you
Have agreed to die?

CHRYSANTHUS.
    'T is true.

ESCARPIN.
Does not this a certain savour
Of insanity give your sadness?

CHRYSANTHUS.
Were I certain as of breath
I could claim it after death,
There was method in my madness.

ESCARPIN.
A brave soldier of the line,
On his death-bed lying ill,
Spoke thus, "Item, 't is my will,
Gallant friends and comrades mine,
That you 'll bear me to my grave,
And although I 've little wealth,
Thirty reals to drink my health
Shall you for your kindness have".
Thus the hope as vain must be
After death one's love to wed,
As to drink one's health when dead.
[Nisida advances from the garden.]

CHRYSANTHUS.
But what maid is this I see
Hither through the garden wending?

ESCARPIN.
If you take a stroll with me

Plenty of her sort you'll see.

NISIDA.
One who would effect the ending
Of thy sadness.

CHRYSANTHUS (aside).
    Now comes near thee,
O my heart, thy threatened trial!
Lady, pardon the denial,
But I would nor see nor hear thee.

NISIDA.
Not so ungallantly surely
Wilt thou act, as not to see
One who comes to speak with thee?

CHRYSANTHUS.
To see one who thinks so poorly
Of herself, and with such lightness
Owns she comes to speak with me,
Rather would appear to be
Want of sense than of politeness.

NISIDA.
All discourse is not so slight
That thou need'st decline it so.

CHRYSANTHUS.
No, I will not see thee, no.
Thus I shut thee from my sight.

NISIDA.

Vainly art thou cold and wise,
Other senses thou shouldst fear,
Since I enter by the ear,
Though thou shut me from the eyes.

Sings.
"The bless`ed rapture of forgetting
Never doth my heart deserve,
What my memory would preserve
Is the memory I 'm regretting".

CHRYSANTHUS.
That melting voice, that melody
Spell-bound holds th' entranc`ed soul.
Ah! from such divine control
Who his fettered soul could free?--
Human Siren, leave me, go!
Too well I feel its fatal power.
I faint before it like a flower
By warm-winds wooed in noontide's glow.
The close-pressed lips the mouth can lock,
And so repress the vain reply,
The lid can veil th' unwilling eye
From all that may offend and shock,--
Nature doth seem a niggard here,
Unequally her gifts disposing,
For no instinctive means of closing
She gives the unprotected ear.

(Enter Cynthia.)

CYNTHIA.
Since then the ear cannot be closed,

The Two Lovers of Heaven: Chrysanthus and Daria

And thou resistance need'st not try,
Listen to the gloss that I
On this sweet conceit composed:
"The bless`ed rapture of forgetting
Never doth my heart deserve;
What my memory would preserve
Is the memory I 'm regretting".
When Nature from the void obscure
Her varied world to life awakes,
All things find use and so endure:--
Thus she a poison never makes
Without its corresponding cure:
Each thing of Nature's careful setting,
Each plant that grows in field or grove
Hath got its opposite flower or weed;
The cure is with the pain decreed;
Thus too is found for feverish love
'The bless`ed rapture of forgetting.'
The starry wonders of the night,
The arbiters of fate on high,
Nothing can dim: To see their light
Is easy, but to draw more nigh
The orbs themselves, exceeds our might.
Thus 't is to know, and only know,
The troubled heart, the trembling nerve,
To sweet oblivion's blank may owe
Their rest, but, ah! that cure of woe
'Never doth my heart deserve.'
Then what imports it that there be,
For all the ills of heart or brain,
A sweet oblivious remedy,
If it, when 't is applied to me,
Fails to cure me of my pain?

Forgetfulness in me doth serve
No useful purpose: But why fret
My heart at this? Do I deserve,
Strange contradiction! to forget
'What my memory would preserve?'
And thus my pain in straits like these,
Must needs despise the only sure
Remedial means of partial ease--
That is--to perish of the cure
Rather than die of the disease.
Then not in wailing or in fretting,
My love, accept thy fate, but let
This victory o'er myself, to thee
Bring consolation, pride, and glee,
Since what I wish not to forget
'Is the memory I 'm regretting.'

CHRYSANTHUS.
'T is not through the voice alone
Music breathes its soft enchantment.[10]
All things that in concord blend
Find in music their one language.
Thou with thy delicious sweetness [To Nisida]
Host my heart at once made captive;--
Thou with thy melodious verses [To Cynthia]
Hast my very soul enraptured.
Ah! how subtly thou dost reason!
Ah! how tenderly thou chantest!
Thou with thy artistic skill,
Thou with thy clear understanding.
But what say I? I speak falsely,
For you both are sphinxes rather,
Who with flattering words seduce me

But to ruin me hereafter:--
Leave me; go: I cannot listen
To your wiles.

NISIDA.
     My lord, oh! hearken
To my song once more.

CYNTHIA.
     Wait! stay!

NISIDA.
Why thus treat with so much harshness
Those who mourn thy deep dejection?

ESCARPIN.
Oh! how soon they 'd have an answer
If they asked of me these questions.
I know how to treat such tattle:
Leave them, sir, to me.

CHRYSANTHUS.
     My senses
'Gainst their lures I must keep guarded:
They are crocodiles, but feigning
Human speech, so but to drag me
To my ruin, my destruction.

NISIDA.
Since my voice will still attract thee,
'T is of little use to fly me.

CYNTHIA.

Though thou dost thy best to guard thee,
While I gloss the words she singeth
To my genius thou must hearken.

CHRYSANTHUS (aside.)
God whom I adore! since I
Help myself, Thy help, oh! grant me!

NISIDA.
"Ah! the joy" .... (she becomes confused.
      But what is this?
Icy torpor coldly fastens
On my hands; the lute drops from me,
And my very breath departeth.

CYNTHIA.
Since she cannot sing; then listen
To this subtle play of fancy:
"Love, if thou 'rt my god" .... (she becomes confused.
      But how,
What can have my mind so darkened
What my memory so confuses,
What my voice can so embarrass?

NISIDA.
I am turned to frost and fire,
I am changed to living marble.

CYNTHIA.
Frozen over is my breast,
And my heart is cleft and hardened.

CHRYSANTHUS.

Thus to lose your wits, ye two,
What can have so strangely happened?

ESCARPIN.
Being poets and musicians,
Quite accounts, sir, for their absence.

NISIDA.
Heavens! beneath the noontide sun
To be left in total darkness!

CYNTHIA.
In an instant, O ye heavens!
O'er your vault can thick clouds gather?

NISIDA.
'Neath the contact of my feet
Earth doth tremble, and I stagger.

CYNTHIA.
Mountains upon mountains seem
On my shoulders to be balanced.

ESCARPIN.
So it always is with those
Who make verses, or who chant them.

CHRYSANTHUS.
Of the one God whom I worship
These are miracles, are marvels.

(Enter Daria.)

DARIA.
Here, Chrysanthus, I have come . . .

NISIDA.
Stay, Daria.

CYNTHIA.
    Stay, 't is rashness
Here to come, for, full of wonders,
Full of terrors is this garden.

ESCARPIN.
Do not enter: awful omens
Threat'ning death await thy advent.

NISIDA.
By my miseries admonished . . . .

CYNTHIA.
By my strange misfortune startled . . .

NISIDA.
Flying from myself, I leave
This green sphere, dismayed, distracted.

CYNTHIA.
Without soul or life I fly,
Overwhelmed by this enchantment.

NISIDA.
Oh! how dreadful!

CYNTHIA.

Oh! how awful!

NISIDA.
Oh! the horror!

CYNTHIA.
    Oh! the anguish! [Exeunt Cynthia and Nisida.]

ESCARPIN.
Mad with jealousy and rage
Have the tuneful twain departed.

DARIA (aside).
Chastisements for due offences
Do not fright me, do not startle,
For if they through arrogance
And ambition sought this garden,
Me the worship of the gods
Here has led, and so I 'm guarded
'Gainst all sorceries whatsoever,
'Gainst all forms of Christian magic:--
Art thou then Chrysanthus?

CHRYSANTHUS.
    Yes.

DARIA.
Not confused or troubled, rather
With a certain fear I see thee,
For which I have grounds most ample.

CHRYSANTHUS.
Why?

DARIA.
>   Because I thought thou wert
One who in a darksome cavern
Died to show thy love for me.

CHRYSANTHUS.
I have yet been not so happy
As to have a chance, Daria,
Of thus proving my attachment.

DARIA.
Be that so, I 've come to seek thee,
Confident, completely sanguine,
That I have the power to conquer,
I alone, thy pains, thy anguish;
Though against me thou shouldst use
The Christian armoury--enchantments.

CHRYSANTHUS.
That thou hast alone the power
To subdue the pains that wrack me,
I admit it; but in what
Thou hast said of Christian magic
I, Daria, must deny it.

DARIA.
How? from what cause else could happen
The effects I just have witnessed?

CHRYSANTHUS.
Miracles they are and marvels.

DARIA.
Why do they affect not me?

CHRYSANTHUS.
'T is because I do not ask them
Against thee; because from aiding
Not myself, no aid is granted.

DARIA.
Then I come here to undo them.

CHRYSANTHUS.
Most severe will be the battle,
Upon one side their due praises
On the other side thy anger.

DARIA.
I would have thee understand
That our gods are sorely damaged
By thy sentiments.

CHRYSANTHUS.
    And I
That those gods are false--mere phantoms.

DARIA.
Then get ready for the conflict,
For I will not lower my standard
Save with victory or death.

CHRYSANTHUS.
Though thou makest me thy captive,
Thou my firmness wilt not conquer.

DARIA.
Then to arms! I say, to arms, then!

CHRYSANTHUS.
Though the outposts of the soul,
The weak heart, by thee be captured;
Not so will the Understanding,
The strong warden who doth guard it.

DARIA.
Thou 'lt believe me, if thou 'lt love me.

CHRYSANTHUS.
Thou not me, 'till love attracts thee.

DARIA.
That perhaps may be; for I
Would not give thee this advantage.

CHRYSANTHUS.
Oh! that love indeed may lead thee
To a state so sweet and happy!

DARIA.
Oh! what power will disabuse thee
Of thy ignorance, Chrysanthus?

CHRYSANTHUS.
Oh! what pitying power, Daria,
Will the Christian faith impart thee?

ACT THE THIRD.

SCENE I.--The Garden of Polemius.

Enter POLEMIUS, AURELIUS, CLAUDIUS, and ESCARPIN.

POLEMIUS.
All my house is in confusion,
Full of terrors, full of horrors;[11]
Ah! how true it is a son
Is the source of many sorrows!--

CLAUDIUS.
But, my lord, reflect . . .

ESCARPIN.
      Consider . . .
Think . . .

POLEMIUS.
      Why think, when misery follows?--
Cease: you add to my affliction,
And in no way bring me solace.
Since you see that in his madness
He is now more firm and constant,
Falling sick of new diseases,
Ere he 's well of old disorders:
Since one young and beauteous maiden,

Whom love wished to him to proffer,
Free from every spot and blemish,
Pure and perfect in her fondness,
Is the one whose fatal charms
Give to him such grief and torment,
That each moment he may perish,
That he may expire each moment;
How then can you hope that I
Now shall list to words of comfort?--

CLAUDIUS.
Why not give this beauteous maiden
To your son to be his consort,
Since you see his inclination?

POLEMIUS.
For this reason: when the project
I proposed, the two made answer,
That before they wed, some problem,
Some dispute that lay between them
Should be settled: this seemed proper:
But when I would know its nature
I could not the cause discover.
From this closeness I infer
That some secret of importance
Lies between them, and that this
Is the source of all my sorrows.

AURELIUS.
Sir, my loyalty, my duty
Will not let me any longer
Silence keep, too clearly seeing
How the evil has passed onward.

On that day we searched the mountain. . . .

POLEMIUS (aside).
Woe is me! could he have known then
All this time it was Chrysanthus?

AURELIUS.
I approaching, where with shoulders
Turned against me stood one figure,
Saw the countenance of another,
And methinks he was . . .

POLEMIUS (aside).
    Ye gods!
Yes, he saw him! help! support me!

AURELIUS.
The same person who came hither
Lately in the garb of a doctor,
Who to-day to cure Chrysanthus
Such unusual treatment orders.
Do you ascertain if he
Is Carpophorus; let no portent
Fright you, on yourself rely,
And you 'll find that all will prosper.

POLEMIUS.
Thanks, Aurelius, for your warning,
Though 't is somewhat tardily offered.
Whether you are right or wrong,
I to-day will solve the problem.
For the sudden palpitation
Of my heart that beats and throbbeth

'Gainst my breast, doth prove how true
Are the suspicions that it fostered.
And if so, then Rome will see
Such examples made, such torments,
That one bleeding corse will show
Wounds enough for myriad corses.   [*Exeunt Aurelius and Polemius.*

CLAUDIUS.
Good Escarpin . . .

ESCARPIN.
      Sir.

CLAUDIUS.
        I know not
How to address you in my sorrow.
Do you say that Cynthia was
One of those not over-modest
Beauties who to court Chrysanthus
Hither came, and who (strange portent!)
Had some share of his bewitchment
In the stupor that came on them?

ESCARPIN.
Yes, sir, and what 's worse, Daria
Was another, thus the torment
That we both endure is equal,
If my case be not the stronger,
Since to love her would be almost
Less an injury than to scorn her.

CLAUDIUS.
Well, I will not quarrel with you

On the point (for it were nonsense)
Whether one should feel more keenly
Love or hate, disdain or fondness
Shown to one we love; enough
'T is to me to know, that prompted
Or by vanity or by interest,
She came hither to hold converse
With him, 't is enough to make me
Lose the love I once felt for her.

ESCARPIN.
Sir, two men, one bald, one squint-eyed,
Met one day . . .

CLAUDIUS.
    What, on your hobby?
A new story?

ESCARPIN.
    To tell stories,
Sir, is not my 'forte', 'pon honour:--
Though who would n't make a hazard
When the ball is over the pocket?--

CLAUDIUS.
Well, I do not care to hear it.

ESCARPIN.
Ah, you know it then: Another
Let me try: A friar once . . .
Stay though, I have quite forgotten
There are no friars yet in Rome:
Well, once more: a fool . . .

CLAUDIUS.
>A blockhead
Like yourself, say: cease.

ESCARPIN.
>Ah, sir,
My poor tale do n't cruelly shorten.
While the sacristan was blowing . . .

CLAUDIUS.
Why, by heaven! I 'll kill you, donkey.

ESCARPIN.
Hear me first, and kill me after.

CLAUDIUS.
Was there ever known such folly
As to think 'mid cares so grave
I could listen to such nonsense? (exit.
[Enter Chrysanthus and Daria, at opposite sides.]

DARIA (to herself).
O ye gods, since my intention
Was in empty air to scatter
All these prodigies and wonders
Worked in favour of Chrysanthus
By the Christians' sorcery, why,
Having you for my copartners,
Do I not achieve a victory
Which my beauty might make facile?

CHRYSANTHUS.

O ye heavens, since my ambition
Was to melt Daria's hardness,
And to bring her to the knowledge
Of one God who works these marvels,
Why, so pure is my intention,
Why, so zealous and so sanguine,
Does not easy victory follow,
Due even to my natural talent?

DARIA (aside).
He is here, and though already
Even to see him, to have parley
With him, lights a living fire
In my breast, which burns yet glads me,
Yet he must confess my gods,
Ere I own that I am vanquished.

CHRYSANTHUS (aside).
She comes hither, and though I
By her beauty am distracted,
Still she must become a Christian
Ere a wife's dear name I grant her.

DARIA (aside).
Venus, to my beauty give
Power to make of him my vassal.

CHRYSANTHUS (aside).
Grant, O Lord, unto my tongue
Words that may dispel her darkness.

DARIA (aside).
To come near him makes me tremble.

CHRYSANTHUS (aside).
To address her, quite unmans me:--
Not in vain, O fair Daria, (aloud.
Does the verdure of this garden,
When it sees thee pass, grow young
As beneath spring's dewy spangles;
Not in vain, since though 't is evening,
Thou a new Aurora dazzleth,
That the birds in public concert
Hail thee with a joyous anthem;
Not in vain the streams and fountains,
As their crystal current passes,
Keep melodious time and tune
With the bent boughs of the alders;
The light movement of the zephyrs
As athwart the flowers they 're wafted,
Bends their heads to see thee coming,
Then uplifts them to look after.

DARIA.
These fine flatteries, these fine phrases
Make me doubt of thee, Chrysanthus.
He who gilds the false so well,
Must mere truth find unattractive.

CHRYSANTHUS.
Hast thou then such little faith
In my love?

DARIA.
      Thou needst not marvel.

CHRYSANTHUS.
Why?

DARIA.
     Because no more of faith
Doth a love deserve that acteth
Such deceptions.

CHRYSANTHUS.
     What deceptions?

DARIA.
Are not those enough, Chrysanthus,
That thou usest to convince me
Of thy love, of thy attachment,
When my first and well-known wishes
Thou perversely disregardest?
Is it possible a man
So distinguished for his talents,
So illustrious in his blood,
Such a favourite from his manners,
Would desire to ruin all
By an error so unhappy,
And for some delusive dream
See himself abhorred and branded?

CHRYSANTHUS.
I nor talents, manners, blood,
Would be worthy of, if madly
I denied a Great First Cause,
Who made all things, mind and matter,
Time, heaven, earth, air, water, fire,
Sun, moon, stars, fish, birds, beasts, Man then.

DARIA.
Did not Jupiter, then, make heaven,
Where we hear his thunders rattle?

CHRYSANTHUS.
No, for if he could have made
Heaven, he had no need to grasp it
For himself at the partition,
When to Neptune's rule he granted
The great sea, and hell to Pluto;--
Then they were ere all this happened.[12]

DARIA.
Is not Ceres the earth, then?

CHRYSANTHUS.
     No.
Since she lets the plough and harrow
Tear its bosom, and a goddess
Would not have her frame so mangled.

DARIA.
Tell me, is not Saturn time?

CHRYSANTHUS.
He is not, though he dispatcheth
All the children he gives birth to;
To a god no crimes should happen.

DARIA.
Is not Venus the air?

CHRYSANTHUS.
> Much less,
Since they say that she was fashioned
From the foam, and foam, we know,
Cannot from the air be gathered.

DARIA.
Is not Neptune the sea?

CHRYSANTHUS.
> As little,
For inconstancy were god's mark then.

DARIA.
Is not the sun Apollo?

CHRYSANTHUS.
> No.

DARIA.
The moon Diana?

CHRYSANTHUS.
> All mere babble.
They are but two shining orbs
Placed in heaven, and there commanded
To obey fixed laws of motion
Which thy mind need not embarrass.
How can these be called the gods--
Gods adulterers and assassins!
Gods who pride themselves for thefts,
And a thousand forms of badness,
If the ideas God and Sin

Are opposed as light to darkness?--
With another argument
I would further sift the matter.
Let then Jupiter be a god,
In his own sphere lord and master:
Let Apollo be one also:
Should Jove wish to hurl in anger
Down his red bolts on the world,
And Apollo would not grant them,
He the so-called god of fire;
From the independent action
Of the two does it not follow
One of them must be the vanquished?
Then they cannot be called gods,
Gods whose wills are counteracted.
One is God whom I adore . . .
And He is, in fine, that martyr
Who has died for love of thee!--
Since then, thou hast said, so adverse
Was thy proud disdain, one only
Thou couldst love with love as ardent
Almost as his own, was he
Who would . . .

DARIA.
      Oh! proceed no farther,
Hold, delay thee, listen, stay,
Do not drive my brain distracted,
Nor confound my wildered senses,
Nor convulse my speech, my language,
Since at hearing such a mystery
All my strength appears departed.
I do not desire to argue

With thee, for, I own it frankly,
I am but an ignorant woman,
Little skilled in such deep matters.
In this law have I been born,
In it have been bred: the chances
Are that in it I shall die:
And since change in me can hardly
Be expected, for I never
At thy bidding will disparage
My own gods, here stay in peace.
Never do I wish to hearken
To thy words again, or see thee,
For even falsehood, when apparelled
In the garb of truth, exerteth
Too much power to be disregarded. [*Exit.*

CHRYSANTHUS.
Stay, I cannot live without thee,
Or, if thou wilt go, the magnet
Of thine eye must make me follow.
All my happiness is anchored
There. Return, Daria. . . .

(*Enter Carpophorus.*)

CARPOPHORUS.
    Stay.
Follow not her steps till after
You have heard me speak.

CHRYSANTHUS.
    What would you?

CARPOPHORUS.
I would reprimand your lapses,
Seeing how ungratefully
You, my son, towards me have acted.

CHRYSANTHUS.
I ungrateful!

CARPOPHORUS.
     You ungrateful,
Yes, because you have abandoned,
Have forgotten God's assistance,
So effectual and so ample.

CHRYSANTHUS.
Do not say I have forgotten
Or abandoned it, wise master,
Since my memory to preserve it
Is as 't were a diamond tablet.

CARPOPHORUS.
Think you that I can believe you,
If when having in this garment
Sought you out to train and teach you,
In the Christian faith and practice,
Until deep theology
You most learnedly have mastered;
If, when having seen your progress,
Your attention and exactness,
I in secret gave you baptism,
Which its mark indelibly stampeth;
You so great a good forgetting,
You for such a bliss so thankless,

With such shameful ease surrender
To this love-dream, this attachment?
Did it strike you not, Chrysanthus,
To that calling how contrasted
Are delights, delirious tumults,
Are love's transports and its raptures,
Which you should resist? Recall too,
Can you not? the aid heaven granted
When you helped yourself, and prayed for
Its assistance: were you not guarded
By it when a sweet voice sung,
When a keen wit glowed and argued,
When the instrument was silenced,
When the tongue was forced to stammer,
Until now, when with free will
You succumb to the enchantment
Of one fair and fatal face,
Which hath done to you such damage
That 't will work your final ruin,
If the trial longer lasteth?--

CHRYSANTHUS.
Oh! my father, oh! my teacher,
Hear me, for although the charges
Brought against me thus are heavy,
Still I to myself have ample
Reasons for my exculpation.
Since you taught me, you, dear master,
That the union of two wills
In our law is well established.
Be not then displeased, Carpophorus . . .
(Aside.) Heavens! what have I said? My father!

(Enter Polemius.)

POLEMIUS (aside).
Ah! this name removes all doubt.
But I must restrain my anger,
And dissemble for the present,
If such patience Jove shall grant me:--
How are you to-day, Chrysanthus? (aloud.

CHRYSANTHUS.
Sir, my love and duty cast them
Humbly at your feet: (aside, Thank heaven,
That he heard me not, this calmness
Cannot be assumed).

POLEMIUS.
  I value
More than I can say your manner
Towards my son, so kind, so zealous
For his health.

CARPOPHORUS.
  Heaven knows, much farther
Even than this is my ambition,
Sir, to serve you: but the passions
Of Chrysanthus are so strong,
That my skill they overmaster.

POLEMIUS.
How?

CARPOPHORUS.
  Because the means of cure

He perversely counteracteth.

CHRYSANTHUS.
Ah! sir, no, I 've left undone
Nothing that you have commanded.

CARPOPHORUS.
No, not so, his greatest peril
He has rashly disregarded.

POLEMIUS.
I implicitly can trust you,
Of whose courage, of whose talents
I have been so well informed,
That I mean at once to grant them
The reward they so well merit.

CARPOPHORUS.
Sir, may heaven preserve and guard you.

POLEMIUS.
Come with me; for I desire
That you should from my apartments
Choose what best doth please you; I
Do not doubt you 'll find an ample
Guerdon for your care.

CARPOPHORUS.
    To be
Honoured in this public manner
Is my best reward.

POLEMIUS (aside).

       The world
Shall this day a dread example
Of my justice see, transcending
All recorded in time's annals. (Exeunt Polemius and Carpophorus.)

CHRYSANTHUS.
Better than I could have hoped for
Has it happened, since my father
Shows by his unruffled face
That his name he has not gathered.
What more evidence can I wish for
Than to see the gracious manner
In which he conducts him whither
His reward he means to grant him?
Oh! that love would do as much
In the fears and doubts that rack me,
Since I cannot wed Daria,
And be faithful to Christ's banner.

(Enter Daria.)

DARIA (aside).
Tyrant question which methought
Timely flight alone could answer,
Once again, against my will
To his presence thou dost drag me.

CHRYSANTHUS (aside).
But she comes again: let sorrow
Be awhile replaced by gladness:--
Ah! Daria, so resolved[13] (aloud,
Not to see or hear me more,
Art thou here?

DARIA.
>Deep pondering o'er,
As the question I revolved,
I would have the mystery solved:
'T is for that I 'm here, then see
It is not to speak with thee.

CHRYSANTHUS.
Speak, what doubt wouldst thou decide?

DARIA.
Thou hast said a God once died
Through His boundless love to me:
Now to bring thee to conviction
Let me this one strong point try . . .

CHRYSANTHUS.
What?

DARIA.
>To be a God, and die,
Doth imply a contradiction.
And if thou dost still deny
To my god the name divine,
And reject him in thy scorn
For beginning, I opine,
If thy God could die, that mine
Might as easily be born.

CHRYSANTHUS.
Thou dost argue with great skill,
But thou must remember still,

That He hath, this God of mine,
Human nature and divine,
And that it has been His will
As it were His power to hide--
God made man--man deified--
When this sinful world He trod,
Since He was not born as God,
And it was as man He died.

DARIA.
Does it not more greatness prove,
As among the beauteous stars,
That one deity should be Mars,
And another should be Jove,
Than this blending God above
With weak man below? To thee
Does not the twin deity
Of two gods more power display,
Than if in some mystic way
God and man conjoined could be?

CHRYSANTHUS.
No, I would infer this rather,
If the god-head were not one,
Each a separate course could run:
But the untreated Father,
But the sole-begotten Son,
But the Holy Spirit who
Ever issues from the two,
Being one sole God, must be
One in power and dignity:--
Until thou dost hold this true,
Till thy creed is that the Son

Was made man, I cannot hear thee,
Cannot see thee or come near thee,
Thee and death at once to shun.

DARIA.
Stay, my love may so be won,
And if thou wouldst wish this done,
Oh! explain this mystery!
What am I to do, ah! me,
That my love may thus be tried?

CARPOPHORUS (within).
Seek, O soul! seek Him who died
Solely for the love of thee.

CHRYSANTHUS.
All that I could have replied
Has been said thus suddenly
By this voice that, sounding near,
Strikes upon my startled ear
Like the summons of my death.

DARIA.
Ah! what frost congeals my breath,
Chilling me with icy fear,
As I hear its sad lament:
Whence did sound the voice? [Enter Polemius and soldiers.

POLEMIUS.
    From here:
'T is, Chrysanthus, my intent
Thus to place before thy sight--
Thus to show thee in what light

I regard thy restoration
Back to health, the estimation
In which I regard the wight
Who so skilfully hath cured thee.
A surprise I have procured thee,
And for him a fit reward:
Raise the curtain, draw the cord,
See, 't is death! If this . . .
(*A curtain is drawn aside, and Carpophorus is seen beheaded, the head being at some distance from the body.*)

CHRYSANTHUS.
     I freeze!--

POLEMIUS.
Is the cure of thy disease,
What must that disease have been!
'T is Carpophorus. . . .

DARIA.
     Dread scene!

POLEMIUS.
He who with false science came
Not to give thee life indeed,
But that he himself should bleed:--
That thy fate be not the same,
Of his mournful end take heed:
Do not thou that dost survive,
My revenge still further drive,
Since the sentence seems misread--
The physician to be dead,
And the invalid alive.--

CHRYSANTHUS.
It were cruelty extreme,
It were some delirious dream,
That could see in this the cure
Of the ill that I endure.

POLEMIUS.
It to him did pity seem,
Seemed the sole reward that he
Asked or would receive from me:
Since when dying, he but cried . .

THE HEAD OF CARPOPHORUS.
Seek, O soul! seek Him who died
Solely for the love of thee!--

CHRYSANTHUS.
What a portent!

DARIA.
    What a wonder!

ESCARPIN.
Jove! my own head splits asunder!--

POLEMIUS.
Even though severed, in it dwells
Still the force of magic spells.

CHRYSANTHUS.
Sir, it were a fatal blunder
To be blind to this appalling

Tragedy you wrong by calling
The result of spells--no spells
Are such signs, but miracles
Outside man's experience falling.
He came here because he yearned
With his pure and holy breath
To give life, and so found death.
'T is a lesson that he learned--
'T is a recompense he earned--
Seeing what his Lord could do,
Being to his Master true:
Kill me also: He had one
Bright example: shall I shun
Death in turn when I have two?

POLEMIUS.
I, in listening to thy raving,
Scarce can calm the wrath thou 'rt braving.
Dead ere now thou sure wouldst lie,
Didst thou not desire to die.

CHRYSANTHUS.
Father, if the death I 'm craving . . .

POLEMIUS.
Speak not thus: no son I know.

CHRYSANTHUS.
Not to thee I spoke, for though
Humanly thou hast that name,
Thou hast forfeited thy claim:
I that sweet address now owe
Unto him whose holier aim

The Two Lovers of Heaven: Chrysanthus and Daria

Kindled in my heart a flame
Which shall there for ever glow,
Woke within me a new soul
That thou 'rt powerless to control--
Generated a new life
Safe against thy hand or knife:
Him a father's name I give
Who indeed has made me live,
Not to him whose tyrant will
Only has the power to kill.
Therefore on this dear one dead,
On this pallid corse laid low,
Lying bathed in blood and snow,
By this lifeless lodestone led,
I such bitter tears shall shed,
That my grief . . .

POLEMIUS.
     Ho! instantly
Tear him from it.

DARIA (aside).
     Thus to be
By such prodigies surrounded,
Leaves me dazzled and confounded.

POLEMIUS.
Hide the corse.

ESCARPIN.
     Leave that to me
(The head and body are concealed).

POLEMIUS.
Bear Chrysanthus now away
To a tower of darksome gloom
Which shall be his living tomb.

CHRYSANTHUS.
That I hear with scant dismay,
Since the memory of this day
With me there will ever dwell.
Fair Daria, fare thee well,
And since now thou knowest who
Died for love of thee, renew
The sweet vow that in the dell
Once thou gav'st me, Him to love
After death who so loved thee.

POLEMIUS.
Take him hence.

DARIA.
    Ah! suddenly
Light descendeth from above
Which my darkness doth remove.
Now thy shadowed truth I see,
Now the Christian's faith profess.
Let thy bloody lictors press
Round me, racking every limb,
Let me only die with him,
Since I openly confess
That the gods are false whom we
Long have worshipped, that I trust
Christ alone--the True--the Just--
The One God, whose power I see,

And who died for love of me.

POLEMIUS.
Take her too, since she in this
Boasts how dark, how blind she is.

DARIA.
Oh! command that I should dwell
With Chrysanthus in his cell.
In our hearts we long are mated,
And ere now had celebrated
Our espousals fond and true,
If the One same God we knew.

CHRYSANTHUS.
This sole bliss alone I waited
To die happy.

POLEMIUS.
    How my heart
Is with wrath and rage possest!--
Hold thy hand, present it not,
For I would not have thy lot
By the least indulgence blest;
Nor do thou, if thy wild brain
Such a desperate course maintain,
Hope to have her as thy bride--
Trophy of our gods denied:--
Separate them.

CHRYSANTHUS.
    O the pain!

DARIA.
O the woe! unhappy me!

POLEMIUS.
Take them hence, and let them be
(Since my justice now at least
Makes amends for mercy past)
Punished so effectually
That their wishes, their desires,
What each wanteth or requires,
Shall be thwarted or denied,
That between opposing fires
They for ever shall be tried:--
Since Chrysanthus' former mood
Only wished the solitude
Whence such sorrows have arisen,
Take him to the public prison,
And be sure in fire and food
That he shall not be preferred
To the meanest culprit there.
Naked, abject, let him fare
As the lowest of the herd:
There, while chains his body gird,
Let him grovel and so die:--
For Daria, too, hard by
Is another public place,
Shameful home of worse disgrace,
Where imprisoned let her lie:
If, relying on the powers
Of her beauty, her vain pride
Dreamed of being my son's bride,
Never shall she see that hour.
Soon shall fade her virgin flower,

Soon be lost her nymph-like grace--
Roses shall desert her face,
Waving gold her silken hair.
She who left Diana's care
Must with Venus find her place:
'Mong vile women let her dwell,
Vile, abandoned even as they.

ESCARPIN (aside).
There my love shall have full play.
O rare judge, you sentence well!

CHRYSANTHUS.
Sir, if thou must have a fell
Vengeance for this act of mine,
Take my life, for it is thine;
But my honour do not dare
To insult through one so fair.

DARIA.
Wreak thy rage, if faith divine
So offends thee, upon me,
Not upon my chastity:--
'T is a virtue purer far
Than the light of sun or star,
And has ne'er offended thee.

POLEMIUS.
Take them hence.

CHRYSANTHUS.
    Ah me, to find
Words, that might affect thy mind!

Melt thy heart!

DARIA.
    Ah, me, who e'er
Saw a martyrdom so rare?--

POLEMIUS.
Wouldst thou then the torment fly,
Thou hast only to deny
Christ.

CHRYSANTHUS.
    The Saviour of mankind?
This I cannot do.

DARIA.
    Nor I.

POLEMIUS.
Let them instantly from this
To their punishment be led.--

ESCARPIN.
Do not budge from what you said.
It is excellent as it is.

CHRYSANTHUS.
Woe is me! but wherefore fear,
O beloved betroth`ed mine?--
Trust in God, that power divine
For whose sake we suffer here:--
HE will aid us and be near:--

DARIA.
In that confidence I live,
For if He His life could give
For my love, and me select,
He His honour will protect.

CHRYSANTHUS.
These sad tears He will forgive.
Ne'er to see thee more! thus driven. . .

DARIA.
Cease, my heart like thine is riven,
But again we 'll see each other,
When in heaven we 'll be, my brother,
The two lover saints of Heaven. (They are led out.

SCENE II.--The hall of a bordel.

Soldiers conducting Daria.

A SOLDIER.
Here Polemius bade us leave her,
The great senator of Rome.[14] (exeunt.)

DARIA.
As the noonday might be left
In the midnight's dusky robe,
As the light amid the darkness,
As 'mid clouds the solar globe:
But although the shades and shadows,

Through the vapours of Heaven's dome.
Strive with villainous presumption
Light and splendour to enfold,
Though they may conceal the lustre,
Still they cannot stain it, no.
And it is a consolation
This to know, that even the gold,
How so many be its carats,
How so rich may be the lode,
Is not certain of its value
'Till the crucible hath told.
Ah! from one extreme to another
Does my strange existence go:
Yesterday in highest honour,
And to-day so poor and low!
Still, if I am self-reliant,
Need I fear an alien foe?
But, ah me, how insufficient
Is my self-defence alone!--
O new God to whom I offer
Life and soul, whom I adore,
In Thy confidence I rest me.
Help me, Lord, I ask no more.

(Enter Escarpin.)

ESCARPIN.
Where I wonder can she be?
But I need not farther go,
Here she is:--At length, Daria,
My good lady, and soforth,
Now has come the happy moment,
When in open market sold,

All thy charms are for the buyer,
Who can spend a little gold;
And since happily love's tariff
Is not an excessive toll,
Here I am, and so, Daria,
Let these clasping arms enfold . . .

DARIA.
Do not Thou desert Thy handmaid
In this dreadful hour, O Lord!--

Cries of people within.

A VOICE (within).
Oh, the lion! oh, the lion!

ANOTHER VOICE (within).
Ho! take care of the lion, ho!

ESCARPIN.
Let the lion care himself,
I 'm engaged and cannot go.

A VOICE (within).
From the mountain wilds descending,
Through the crowded streets he goes.

ANOTHER VOICE (within).
Like the lightning's flash he flieth,
Like the thunder is his roar.

ESCARPIN.
Ah! all right, for I 'm in safety,

Thanks to this obliging door:
Lightning is a thing intended
For high towers and stately domes,
Never heard I of its falling
Upon little lowly homes:
So if lion be the lightning,
Somewhere else will fall the bolt:
Therefore once again, Daria,
Come, I say, embrace me. . . . .
(A lion enters, places himself before Daria, and seizes Escarpin.)

DARIA.
     Oh!
Never in my life did I
See a nobler beast.

ESCARPIN.
     Just so,
Nor a more affectionate one
Did I ever meet before,
Since he gives me the embraces
That I asked of thee and more:
O god Bacchus, whom I worship
So devoutly, thou, I know,
Workest powerfully on beasts.
Tell our friend to let me go.

DARIA.
Noble brute, defend my honour,
Be God's minister below.

ESCARPIN.
How he gnaws me! how he claws me!

How he smells! His breath, by Jove,
Is as bad as an emetic.
But you need n't eat me, though.
That would be a sorry blunder,
Like what happened long ago.
Would you like to hear the story?
By your growling you say no.
What! you 'll eat me then? You 'll find me
A tough morsel, skin and bone.
O Daria! I implore thee,
Save me from this monster's throat,
And I give to thee my promise
To respect thee evermore.

DARIA.
Mighty monarch of these deserts,
King of beasts, so plainly known
By thy crown of golden tresses
O'er thy tawny forehead thrown,
In the name of Him who sent thee
To defend that faith I hold,
I command thee to release him,
Free this man and let him go.

ESCARPIN.
What a most obsequious monster!
With his mane he sweeps the floor,
And before her humbly falling,
Kisses her fair feet.

DARIA.
    What more
Need we ask, that Thou didst send him,

O great God so late adored,
Than to see his pride thus humbled
When he heard thy name implored?
But upon his feet uprising,
The great roaring Campeador[15]
Of the mountains makes a signal
I should follow: yes, I go,
Fearless now since Thou hast freed me
From this infamous abode.
What will not that lover do
Who for love his life foregoes!-- (Goes out preceded by the lion.

ESCARPIN.
With a lion for her bully
Ready to fight all her foes,
Who will dare to interrupt her?
None, if they are wise I trow.
With her hand upon his mane,
Quite familiarly they go
Through the centre of the city.
Crowds give way as they approach,
And as he who looketh on
Knoweth of the game much more
Than the players, I perceive
They the open country seek
On the further side of Rome.
Like a husband and a wife,
In the pleasant sunshine's glow,
Taking the sweet air they seem.
Well the whole affair doth show
So much curious contradiction,
That, my thought, a brief discourse
You and I must have together.

Is the God whose name is known
To Daria, the same God
Whom Carpophorus adored?
Why, from this what inference follows?
Only this, if it be so,
That Daria He defends,
But the poor Carpophorus, no.
And as I am much more likely
His sad fate to undergo,
Than to be like her protected,
I to change my faith am loth.
So part pagan and part christian
I 'll remain--a bit of both. (Exit.

SCENE III.--The Wood.

(Enter NISIDA and CYNTHIA, flying.)

CYNTHIA.
Fly, fly, Nisida.

NISIDA.
    Fly, fly, Cynthia,
Since a terror and a woe
Threatens us by far more fearful
Than when late a horror froze
All our words, and o'er our reason
Strange lethargic dulness flowed.

CYNTHIA.

Thou art right, for then 't was only
Our intelligence that owned
The effect of an enchantment,
A mere pause of thought alone.
Here our very life doth leave us,
Seeing with what awful force
Stalks along this mighty lion
Trampling all that stops his course.

NISIDA.
Whither shall we fly for shelter?

CYNTHIA.
O Diana, we implore
Help from thee! But stranger still!--
Him who doth appal us so,
The wild monarch of the mountain
See! a woman calm and slow
Follows.

NISIDA.
     O astounding sight!

CYNTHIA.
'T is Daria.

NISIDA.
     I was told
She had been consigned to prison:
Yes, 't is she: on, on they go
Through the forest.

CYNTHIA.

             Till the mountain
Hides them, and we see no more.

(Enter Escarpin.)

ESCARPIN.
All Rome is full of wonder and dismay.[16]

NISIDA.
What has occurred?

CYNTHIA.
            Oh! what has happened, say?

ESCARPIN.
Chrysanthus, being immured
By his stern sire, a thousand ills endured.
Daria too, the same,
But in a house my tongue declines to name.
It pleased the God they both adore
Both to their freedom strangely to restore,
And from their many pains
To free them, and to break their galling chains,
Giving Daria, as attendant squire,
A roaring lion, rolling eyes of fire:--
In fine the two have fled,
But each apart by separate instinct led
To this wild mountain near.
Numerianus coming then to hear
Of the event, assuming in his wrath,
That 't was Polemius who had oped the path
Of freedom for his son and for the maid,
Has not an hour delayed,

But follows them with such a numerous band,
That, see, his squadrons cover all the land.

VOICES (within).
Scour the whole plain.

OTHERS (within).
     Descend into the vale.

OTHERS (within).
Pierce the thick wood.

OTHERS (within).
     The rugged mountain scale.

ESCARPIN.
This noise, these cries, confirm what I have said:
And since by curiosity I 'm led
To sift the matter to the bottom, I
Will follow with the rest.

CYNTHIA.
     I almost die
With fear at the alarm, and yet so great
Is my desire to know Daria's fate,
And that of young Chrysanthus, that I too
Will follow, if a woman so may do.

ESCARPIN.
What strange results such strange events produce!
The very wonder serves as an excuse.

NISIDA.

Well, we must only hope that it is so.
Come, Cynthia, let us follow her.

CYNTHIA.
>Let us go.

ESCARPIN.
And I with love most fervent,
Ladies, will be your very humble servant. [Exeunt.

SCENE IV.--A wilder part of the wood near the cave.

(Enter DARIA guided by the lion.)

DARIA.
O mighty lion, whither am I led?
Where wouldst thou guide me with thy stately tread,
That seems to walk not on the earth, but air?
But lo! he has entered there
Where yonder cave its yawning mouth lays bare,

[The lion enters a cave.]

Leaving me here alone.
But now fate clears, and all will soon be known;
For if I read aright
The signs this desert gives unto my sight,
It is the very place whence echo gave
Responsive music from this mystic cave.
Terror and wonder both my senses scare,

Ah! whither shall I go?

CHRYSANTHUS (within).
    Daria fair!

DARIA.
Who calls my hapless name?
Each leaf that moves doth thrill this wretched frame
With boding and with dread.
But why say wretched? I had better said
Thrice bless`ed: O great God whom I adore,
Baptize me in those tears that I outpour,
In no more fitting form can I declare
My faith and hope in thee.

CHRYSANTHUS (within).
    Daria fair.

DARIA.
Who calls my name? who wakes those wild alarms?

(Enter Chrysanthus.)

CHRYSANTHUS.
Belov`ed bride, 't is one to whom thy charms
Are even less dear than is thy soul, ah! me,
One who would live and who will die with thee.

DARIA.
Belov`ed spouse, my heart could not demand
Than thus to see thee near, to clasp thy hand,
A sweeter solace for my long dismay,
And all the awful wonders of this day.

Hear the surprising tale,
And thou wilt know . . .

VOICES (within).
  Search hill.

OTHERS.
  And plain.

OTHERS.
  And vale.

CHRYSANTHUS.
Hush! the troops our fight pursuing
Have the forest precincts entered.[17]

DARIA.
What then shall I do, Chrysanthus?

CHRYSANTHUS.
Keep thy faith, thy life surrender:--

DARIA.
I a thousand lives would offer:
Since to God I 'm so indebted
That I 'll think myself too happy
If 't is given for Him.

POLEMIUS (within).
  This centre
Of the mountain, whence the sun
Scarcely ever is reflected--
This dark cavern sure must hold them.

Let us penetrate its entrails,
So that here the twain may die.

DARIA.
One thing only is regretted
By me, in my life thus losing,
I am not baptized.

CHRYSANTHUS.
     Reject then
That mistrust; in blood and fire[18]
Martyrdom the rite effecteth:--

(Enter Polemius and Soldiers.)

POLEMIUS.
Here, my soldiers, here they are,
And the hand that death presents them
Must be mine, that none may think
I a greater love could cherish
For my son than for my gods.
And as I desire, when wendeth
Hither great Numerianus,
That he find them dead, arrest them
On the spot, and fling them headlong
Into yonder cave whose centre
Is a fathomless abyss:--
And since one sole love cemented
Their two hearts in life, in death
In one sepulchre preserve them.

CHRYSANTHUS.
Oh! how joyfully I die!

DARIA.
And I also, since the sentence
Gives to me the full assurance
Of a happiness most certain
On the day this darksome cave
Doth entomb me in its centre. (They are cast into the abyss.)

POLEMIUS.
Cover the pit's mouth with stones.
(A sudden storm of thunder and lightning: Enter Numerianus, Claudius, Aurelius, and others.

NUMERIANUS.
What can have produced this tempest?

POLEMIUS.
When within the cave they threw them,
Dark eclipse o'erspread the heavens.

CLAUDIUS.
Shadowy shapes, phantasmal shadows
Are upon the wind projected.

CYNTHIA.
Lightnings like swift birds of fire
Dart along with burning tresses.

CLAUDIUS.
Lo! an earthquake's awful shudder
Makes the very mountains tremble.

POLEMIUS.

Yes, the solid ground upheaveth,
And the mighty rock descendeth
O'er our heads.

NISIDA.
     While on the instant
Dulcet voices soft and tender
Issue from the cave's abysses.

NUMERIANUS.
Rome to-day strange sights presenteth,
When a grave exhibits gladness,
And the sun displays resentment.

(A choir of angels is heard singing from within the cave.)
"Happy day, and happy doom,
May the gladsome world exclaim,
When the darksome cave became
Saint Daria's sacred tomb".
(A great rock falls from the mountain, and covers the tomb, over it is seen an angel.)

ANGEL.
This great cave which holds to-day
In its breast so great a treasure,
Never shall by foot be trodden;--
Thus it is I 've sealed and settled
This great mass of rock upon it,
Which doth shut it up for ever.
And in order that their ashes
On the wind be ne'er dispers`ed,
But while time itself endureth
Shall be honoured and respected,

This brief epitaph, this simple
Line shall tell this simple legend
To the ages that come after:
"Here the bodies are preserv`ed
Of Chrysanthus and Daria,
The two lover-saints of Heaven".

CLAUDIUS.
Wherefore humbly we entreat
Pardon for our many errors.

3. The whole of the first scene is in 'asonante' verse, the vowels being i, e, as in "restrIctEd", "drIftlEss", "hIddEn", etc. These vowels, or their equivalents in sound, will be found pretty accurately represented in the last two syllables of every alternate line throughout the scene, which ends at p. 25, and where the verse changes into the full consonant rhyme.

4. The resemblance between certain parts of Goethe's Faust and The Wonder-Working Magician of Calderon has been frequently alluded to, and has given rise to a good deal of discussion. In the controversy as to how much the German poet was indebted to the Spanish, I do not recollect any reference to The Two Lovers of Heaven. The following passage, however, both in its spirit and language, presents a singular likeness to the more elaborate discussion of the same difficulty in the text. The scene is in Faustus's study. Faustus, as in the present play, takes up a volume of the New Testament, and thus proceeds:

"IN THE BEGINNING WAS THE WORD". Alas!
The first line stops me: how shall I proceed?

"The word" cannot express the meaning here.
I must translate the passage differently,
If by the spirit I am rightly guided.
Once more,--"IN THE BEGINNING WAS THE THOUGHT".--
Consider the first line attentively,
Lest hurrying on too fast, you lose the meaning.
Was it then Thought that has created all things?
Can thought make matter? Let us try the line
Once more,--"IN THE BEGINNING WAS THE POWER"--
This will not do--even while I write the phrase,
I feel its faults--oh! help me, holy Spirit,
I 'll weigh the passage once again, and write
Boldly,--"IN THE BEGINNING WAS THE ACT".
  Anster's "Faustus", Francfort ed., 1841, p. 63.

5. The same line of argument is worked out with wonderful subtlety of thought and beauty of poetical expression by Calderon, in one of the finest of his Autos Sacramentales, "The Sacred Parnassus". Autos Sacramentales, tom. vi. p. 10.

6. The metre reverts here again to the asonante form, which is kept up for the remainder of this act. The vowels here used are e, e, or their equivalents.

7. "This Clytie knew, and knew she was undone,
  Whose soul was fix'd, and doted on the sun".
  OVID, Metamorphoses, b. iv.

8. In the whole of this scene the asonante vowels are a-e, or their equivalents.

9. The asonante in e-e, recommences here, and continues until the entry of Chrysanthus.

10. The metre changes to the asonante in a-e for the remainder of this Act.

11. The asonante in this scene is generally in o-e, o-o, o-a, which are nearly all alike in sound. In the second scene the asonante is in a-e, as in "scAttEr", etc.

12. See note referring to the auto, "The Sacred Parnassus", Act 1, p. 21.

13. The asonante changes here into five-lined stanzas in ordinary rhyme. Three lines rhyme one way and two the other. Poems in this metre are called in Spanish 'Versos de arte mayor,' from the greater skill supposed to be required for their composition.

14. The asonante is single here, consisting only of the long accented o, as in "ROme", "glObe", "dOme", etc.

15. Champion, or combater, the name generally given the Cid.

16. The metre changes to an irregular couplet in long and short lines.

17. The metre changes to the double asonante in e-e, which continues to the end of the drama.

18. Baptism by blood and fire through martyrdom. Calderon refers here evidently to the words of St. John the Baptist: "He shall baptize you in the Holy Ghost and fire"--St. Matth., c. iii. v. ii. The following passage in the Legend of St. Catherine must also have been present to his mind:

"Et cum dolerent, quod sine baptismo decederent, virgo respondit: Ne timeatis, quia effusio vestri sanguinis vobis baptismus reputabitur et corona". Legenda Aurea, c. 167.

THE SPANISH DRAMA.

CALDERON'S DRAMAS AND AUTOS,

Translated into English Verse
BY DENIS FLORENCE MAC-CARTHY.

From Ticknor's History of Spanish Literature. London: 1863.

"Denis Florence M'Carthy published in London (in 1861) translations of two plays, and an auto of Calderon, under the title of 'Love, the greatest Enchantment; the Sorceries of Sin; the Devotion of the Cross, from the Spanish of Calderon, attempted strictly in English Asonante, and other imitative Verse', printing, at the same time, a carefully corrected text of the originals, page by page, opposite to his translations. It is, I think, one of the boldest attempts ever made in English verse. It is, too, as it seems to me, remarkably successful. Not that asonantes can be made fluent or graceful in English, or easily perceptible to an English ear, but that the Spanish air and character of Calderon are so happily preserved. Mr. M'Carthy, in 1853, had published two volumes of translations from Calderon, to which I have already referred; and, besides this, he has rendered excellent service to the cause of Spanish literature in other ways. But in the present volume he has far surpassed all he had previously done; for Calderon is a poet who, whenever he is translated, should have his very excesses, both in thought and manner, fully produced, in order to give a faithful idea of what is grandest and most distinctive in his genius. Mr. M'Carthy has done this, I conceive, to a degree which I had previously considered impossible. Nothing, I think, in the English language will give us so true an impression of what is most characteristic of the Spanish drama; perhaps I ought to say, of what is most characteristic of Spanish poetry generally".--tom. iii. pp. 461, 462.

Extracts from Continental Reviews.

From "Blaeater fuer Literarische Unterhaltung". 1862. Erster Baude, 479 Leipzig, F. A. Brockhans.

"Erwaehnenswerth ist folgender Kuehne versuch einer Rachdildung Calderon' scher stuecke in Englishchen Assonanzen.

"Love, the greatest enchantment; The Sorceries of Sin; The Devotion of the Cross, from the Spanish of Calderon, attempted strictly in English Asonante, and other imitative verse. By Denis Florence Mac-Carthy".

Diese Uebersetzung ist dem Verfasser der "History of Spanish Literature", George Ticknor, zugeeignet, der in einem Schreiber au den Uebersetzer die Arbeit "marvellous" nennt und dam fortfaehrt:

"Richt das sie die Assonanzen dem englischen Ohr so hoerbar gemacht haetten, wie dies mit den Spanischen der Fall ist; unsere widerhaarigen consonanten machen dies unmoeglich; das Wunderbare ist nur, das sie dieselben ueberhaupt hoerbar gemacht haben. Meiner Meinung nach nehme ist Ihre Assonanzen so deutlich wahr, wil die Von August Schlegel oder

Gries und mehr als diejenigen Friedrich Schlegel's. Aber dieser war der erste, der den versuch dazu machte, und ausserdem bin ich Kein Deutscher. Wurde es nicht lustig sein, wenn man einmal ein solches Experiment in franzoeschicher Sprache wolte?"

"Ohne zweifel wuerde MacCarthy Ohne den vorgaug deutscher Nachbilder des Calderon ebenso wenig darauf gekommen sein englische Assonanzen zu versuchen, als man ohne das ermunternde Beispiel deutscher Dichter und Uebersetzer darauf gekommen sein wurde, in Uebersetzungen und originaldichtungen unter welchen letztern wol besonders Longfellow's 'Evangeline', zu nennen ist, englische Hexameter zu versuchen, was in letzter zeit gar nicht selten geschehen ist".

From "Boletin de Ferro-Carriles". Cadiz: 1862.

"La novedad que nos comunica de la existencia de traducciones tan acabadas de nuestro grande e inimitable Calderon, ostendando, hasta cierto punto, las galas y formas del original, estamos seguros sera acogida con favor, si no con entusiasmo, per los verdaderos amantes de las letras espanolas. A ellos nos dirijimos, recomendandoles el ultimo trabajo del Senor Mac-Carthy, seguros de que participaran del mismo placer que nosotros hemos experimentado al examinar su fiel, al par que brillante traduccion; y en cuanto a la dificil tentativa de los asonantes ingleses, nos sorpende que el Senor Mac-Carthy haya podido sacar tanto parido, si se considera la indole peculiar de los dos idiomas".

Extracts from Letters addressed to the Author.

From Henry Wadsworth Longfellow, Esq.
Cambridge, near Boston, America, April 29, 1862.

"I thank you very much for your new work in the vast and flowery fields of Calderon. It is, I think, admirable; and presents the old Spanish dramatist before the English reader in a very attractive light.

"Particularly in the most poetical passages you are excellent; as, for instance, in the fine description of the gerfalcon and the heron in 'El Mayor Encanto'.--11 Jor.

"Your previous volumes I have long possessed and highly prized; and I hope you mean to add more and more, so as to make the translation as nearly complete as a single life will permit. It seems rather appalling to undertake the whole of so voluminous a writer. Nevertheless, I hope you will do it. Having proved that you can, perhaps you ought to do it. This may be your appointed work. It is a noble one.

"With much regard, I am, etc.,
"HENRY W. LONGFELLOW.

"Denis Florence Mac-Carthy, Esq.".

From the Same.
Nahant, near Boston, August 10, 1857.

"MY DEAR SIR,

"Before leaving Cambridge to come down here to the sea-side, I had the pleasure of receiving your precious volume of 'Mysteries of Corpus Christi'; and should have thanked you sooner for your kindness in sending it to me, had I not been very busy at the time in getting out my last volume of Dante.

"I at once read your work, with eagerness and delight--that peculiar and strange delight which Calderon gives his admirers, as peculiar and distinct as the flavour of an olive from that of all other fruits.

"You are doing this work admirably, and seem to gain new strength and sweetness as you go on. It seems as if Calderon himself were behind you whispering and suggesting. And what better work could you do in your bright hours or in your dark hours than just this, which seems to have been put providentially into your hands!

"The extracts from the 'Sacred Parnassus' in the Chronicle, which reached me yesterday, are also excellent.

"For this and all, many and many thanks.

"Yours faithfully,
"HENRY W. LONGFELLOW.

"Denis Florence Mac-Carthy, Esq.".

From George Ticknor, Esq., the Historian of Spanish Literature.
"Boston, 16th December, 1861.

"In this point of view, your volume seems to me little less than marvellous. If I had not read it--indeed, if I had not carefully gone through with the "Devocion de la Cruz", I should not have believed it possible to do what you have done. Titian, they say, and some others of the old masters, laid on colours for their groundwork wholly different from those they used afterwards, but which they counted upon to shine through, and contribute materially to the grand results they produced.

So in your translations, the Spanish seems to come through to the surface; the original air is always perceptible in your variations. It is like a family likeness coming out in the next generation, yet with the freshness of originality.

"But the rhyme is as remarkable as the verse and the translation; not that you have made the asonante as perceptible to the English ear as it is to the Spanish; our cumbersome consonants make that impossible. But the wonder is, that you have made it perceptible at all. I think I perceive your asonantes much as I do those of August Schlegel or Gries, and more than I do those of Friederich Schlegel. But he was the first who tried them, and, besides, I am not a German. Would it not be amusing to have the experiment tried in French?"

From the Same.
"Boston, March 20, 1867.

"The world has claims on you which you ought not to evade; and, if the path in which you walk of preference, leads to no wide popularity or brilliant profits, it is, at least, one you have much to yourself, and cannot fail to enjoy. You have chosen it from faithful love, and will always love it; I suspect partly because it is your own choice, because it is peculiarly your own".

From the Same.
"Boston, July 3, 1867.

"Considered from this point of view, I think that in your present volume ["Mysteries of Corpus Christi", or "Autos Sacramentales" of Calderon] you are always as successful as you were in your previous publications of the same sort, and sometimes more so; easier, I mean, freer, and more happily expressive. If I were to pick out my first preference, I should take your fragment of the 'Veneno y Triaca', at the end; but I think the whole volume is more fluent, pleasing, and attractive than even its predecessors".

From the first of English religious painters.

"I cannot resist the impulse I have of offering you my most grateful thanks for the greatest intellectual treat I have ever experienced in my life, and which you have afforded me in the magnificent translations of the divine Calderon; for, surely, of all the poets the world ever saw, he alone is worthy of standing beside the author of the Book of Job and of the Psalms, and entrusted, like them, with the noble mission of commending to the hearts of others all that belongs to the beautiful and true, ever directing the thoughtful reader through the love of the beautiful veil, to the great Author of all perfection.

"I cannot conceive a nation can receive a greater boon than being helped to a love of such works as the religious dramas of this Prince of Poets. I have for years felt this, and as your translations appeared, have read them with the greatest possible interest. I knew not of the publication of the last, and it was to an accidental, yet, with me, habitual outburst of praise of Calderon, as the antidote and cure for the trifling literature of the day, that my friend (the) D---- made me aware of its being out".

[The work especially referred to in the latter part of this interesting letter is the following: "Mysteries of Corpus Christi (Autos Sacramentales), from the Spanish of Calderon, by Denis Florence Mac-Carthy". Duffy, Dublin and London, 1867.]

The Two Lovers of Heaven: Chrysanthus and Daria

Extracts from American and Canadian Journals.

From an eloquent article in the "Boston Courier", March 18, 1862, written by George Stillman Hillard, Esq., the author of "Six Months in Italy"--a delightful book, worthy of the beautiful country it so beautifully describes.

"Calderon is one of the three greatest names in Spanish literature, Lope de Vega and Cervantes being the other two. He is also a great name in the universal realm of letters, though out of Spain he is little more than a great name, except in Germany, that land so hospitable to famous wits, and where, to readers and critics of a mystical and transcendental turn, his peculiar genius strongly commended him. To form a notion of what manner of man Calderon was, we must imagine a writer hardly inferior to Shakespeare in fertility of invention and dramatic insight, inspired by a religious fervour like that of Doune or Crashaw, and endowed with the wild and ethereal imagination of Shelley. But the religious fervour is Catholic, not Protestant, Southern, not Northern: it is intense, mystical, and ecstatic: like a tongue of upward-darting flame, it burns and trembles with impassioned impulse to mingle with empyrean fire. The imagination, too, is not merely southern, but with an oriental element shining through it, like the ruddy heart of an opal". . .

"But our purpose is not to speak of Calderon, but of his translator Mr. MacCarthy; and to make our readers acquainted with his very successful effort to reproduce in English some of the most characteristic productions of the genius of Spain, retaining even one of the peculiarities in the structure of the verse which has hardly ever been transplanted from the soil of the peninsula". . . .

"Mr. MacCarthy's translations strike us as among the most successful experiments which have been made to represent in our language the characteristic beauties of the finest productions of other nations. They are sufficiently faithful, as may be readily seen by the Spanish scholar, as the translator has the courage to print the original and his version side by side. The rich, imaginative passages of Calderon are reproduced in language of such grace and flexibility as shows in Mr. MacCarthy no inconsiderable amount of poetical power. The measures of Calderon are retained; the rhymed passages are translated into rhyme, and what is more noticeable still, Mr. MacCarthy has done what no writer in English has ever before essayed, except to a very limited extent--he has copied the asonantes of the original". . . .

"We take leave of Mr. MacCarthy with hearty acknowledgments for the pleasure we have had in reading his excellent translations, which have given us a sense of Calderon's various and brilliant genius such as we never before had, and no analysis of his dramas, however full and careful, could bestow".

From a Review of "Love the Greatest Enchantment", etc., in the "New York Tablet", July 19, 1862, written by the gifted and ill-fated Hon. Thomas D'Arcy M'Gee, of Montreal.

"This beautiful volume before us--like virtue's self, fair within and without--is Mr. Mac-Carthy's second contribution to the Herculean task which Longfellow cheers him on to continue--the translation into English of the complete works of Calderon. Two experimental volumes, containing six dramas of the same author, appeared in 1853, winning the well-merited encomium of every person of true taste into whose hands they happened to fall. The Translator was encouraged, if not by the general chorus of popular applause, by the precious and emphatic approbation of those best entitled by knowledge and accomplishments to pronounce judgment. So here, after an interval of seven years, we have right worthily presented to us three of those famous Autos, which for two centuries drew together all the multitude of the Madrilenos, on the annual return of the great feast of Corpus Christi. On that same self-same festival, in a northern land, under a gray and clouded sky, in the heart of a city most unlike gay, garden-hued, out-of-door Madrid, we have spent the long hours over these resurrected dramas, and the spell of both the poets is still upon us, as we unite together, in dutiful juxtaposition, the names of Calderon and Mac-Carthy.

"How richly gifted was this Spanish priest-poet! this pious playwright! this moral mechanist! this devout dramatist! How rare his experience! how broad the contrasts of his career, and of his observation. . . . . Happy poet! blessed with such fecundity! Happy Christian! blessed with such fidelity to the divine teachings of the Cross. . . .

"Very highly do we reverence Calderon, and very highly value his translator; yet, if it be not presumptuous to say so, we venture to suggest that Mac-Carthy might find nearer home another work still worthier of his genius than these translations. Now that he has got the imperial ear by bringing his costly wares from afar, are there not laurels to be gathered as well in Ireland as in Spain? The author of 'The Bell-Founder', of 'St. Brendan's Voyage', of 'The Foray of Con O'Donnell', and 'The Pillar Towers', needs no prompting to discern what abundant materials for a new department of English poetry are to be found almost unused on Irish ground. May we not hope that in that field or forest he may find his appointed work, adding to the glory of first worthily introducing Calderon to the English readers of this century, the still higher glory of doing for the neglected history of his fatherland what he has chivalrously done for the illustrious Spaniard".

A LIST
OF
Calderon's Dramas and Autos Sacramentales,

Translated into English Verse
BY DENIS FLORENCE MAC-CARTHY, M.R.I.A.

THE PURGATORY OF SAINT PATRICK.

"With the 'Purgatory of St. Patrick' especial pains seem to have been taken".

"Considerable license has been taken with the prayer of St. Patrick; but its spirit is well preserved, and the translator's poetry must be admired".

"If Calderon can ever be made popular here, it must be in the manner generally adopted by Mr. Mac-Carthy in the specimens, six in number, which are here translated, preserving, namely, the metrical form, which is one of the characteristics of the old Spanish drama. This medium, through which it partakes of the lyrical character, is no accident of style, but an essential property of that remarkable creation of a poetic age--remarkable, because while the drama so adorned was entirely the offspring of popular impulse, in opposition to many rigorous attempts in favour of classical methods, it was at the same time raised above the tone of common expression by the rhythmical mode which it assumed, in a manner decisive of its ideal tendency. It thus displays a combination rare in this kind of poetry: the spirit of an untutored will, embodied in a form the romantic expression of which might seem only congenial to choice and delicate fancies. . . . .

"In conclusion, what has now been said of Calderon, and of the stage which he adorned, as well as of the praise justly due to parts of Mr. Mac-Carthy's version, will at least serve to commend these volumes to curious lovers of poetry".

From an elaborate article in "The Athenaeum", by the late eminent Spanish scholar, Mr. J. R. Chorley, on the first two volumes of Mr. Mac-Carthy's translations from Calderon.

THE CONSTANT PRINCE.

A Drama.

"In his dramas of a serious and devout character, in virtue of their dignified pathos, tragic sublimity, and religious fervour, Calderon's best title to praise will be found. In such, above all in his Autos, he reached a height beyond any of his predecessors, whose productions, on religious themes especially, striking as many of them are, with situations and motives of the deepest effect, are not sustained at the same impressive elevation, nor disposed with that consummate judgment which leaves nothing imperfect or superfluous in the dramas of Calderon. 'The Constant Prince' and 'The Physician of his own Honour', which Mr. Mac-Carthy has translated, are noble instances representing two extremes of a large class of dramas".

From the same article in "The Athenaeum", by J. R. Chorley.

THE PHYSICIAN OF HIS OWN HONOUR.

"'The Physician of his own Honour' is a domestic tragedy, and must be one of the most fearful to witness ever brought upon the stage. The highest excess of dramatic powers, terror and gloom has certainly been reached in this drama".

From an eloquent article in "The Dublin University Magazine" on "D. F. Mac-Carthy's Calderon".

THE SECRET IN WORDS.

A Drama.

"The ingenious verbal artifice of 'The Secret in Words', although a mere trifle if compared to the marvellous intricacy of a similar cipher in Tirso's 'Amar por Arte Mayor', from which Calderon's play was taken--loses sadly in a translation; yet the piece, even with this disadvantage, cannot fail to please".

J. R. Chorley in "The Athenaeum".

THE SCARF AND THE FLOWER.

A Drama.

"The 'Scarf and the Flower', nice and courtly though it be, the subject spun out and entangled with infinite skill, is too thin by itself for an interest of three acts long; and no translation, perhaps, could preserve the grace of manner and glittering flow of dialogue which conceal this defect in the original".

J. R. Chorley in "The Athenaeum".

LOVE AFTER DEATH.

A Drama.

"'Love after Death' is a drama full of excitement and beauty, of passion and power, of scenes whose enthusiastic affection, self-devotion, and undying love are drawn with more intense colouring than we find in any other of Calderon's works".

From an article in "The Dublin University Magazine" on D. F. Mac-Carthy's Calderon.

"Another tragedy, 'Love after Death', is connected with the hopeless rising of the Moriscoes in the Alpujarras (1568-1570), one of whom is its hero. It is for many reasons worthy of note; amongst others, as showing how far Calderon could rise above national prejudices, and expend all the treasures of his genius in glorifying the heroic devotedness of a noble foe".

Archbishop Trench.

LOVE THE GREATEST ENCHANTMENT

A Drama.

"This fact connects the piece with the first and most pleasing in the volume, 'Love the greatest Enchantment', in which the same myth [that of Circe and Ulysses] is exhibited in a more life-like form, though not without some touches of allegory. Here we have a classical plot which is adapted to the taste of Spain in the seventeenth century by a plentiful admixture of episodes of love and gallantry. The adventure is opened with nearly the same circumstances as in the tenth Odyssey: but from the moment that Ulysses, with the help of a divine talisman, has frustrated all the spells (beauty excepted) of the enchantress, the action is adapted to the manners of a more refined and chivalrous circle".

"The Saturday Review" in its review of "Mac-Carthy's Three Plays of Calderon".

THE DEVOTION OF THE CROSS.

A Drama.

"The last drama to which Mr. Mac-Carthy introduces us is the famous 'Devotion of the Cross'. We cannot deny the praise of great power to this strange and repulsive work, in which Calderon draws us onward by a deep and terrible dramatic interest, while doing cruel violence to our moral nature. . . . Our readers may be glad to compare the translations which Archbishop Trench and Mr. Mac-Carthy have given us of a celebrated address to the Cross contained in this drama. 'Tree whereon the pitying skies', etc. Mr. Mac-Carthy does not appear to us to suffer from comparison on this occasion with a true poet, who is also a skilful translator. Indeed he has faced the difficulties and given the sense of the original with more decision than Archbishop Trench".

"The Guardian", in its review of the same volume.

THE SORCERIES OF SIN.

An Auto.

"The central piece, the 'Sorceries of Sin', is an 'Auto Sacramental', or Morality, of which the actors represent Man, Sin, Voluptuousness, etc., Understanding, and the Five Senses. The Senses are corrupted by the influence of Sin, and figuratively changed into wild beasts. Man, accompanied by Understanding and Penance, demands their liberation and encounters no resistance; but his free-will is afterwards seduced by the Evil Power, and his allies reclaim him with difficulty. Yet the plan of the apologue is embellished with many ingenious conceits and artifices, and conformed in the leading circumstances with an Homeric myth--the names of Ulysses and Circe being frequently substituted for those of the Man and Sin".

"The Saturday Review" on "Mac-Carthy's Three Plays of Calderon".

BELSHAZZAR'S FEAST.

An Auto.

"The first auto translated is 'Belshazzar's Feast', a fortunate selection, for it is probably unsurpassed in dramatic effect and poetic description, and withal is much less encumbered with theology than most others".

From an article in "The New York Nation", by a distinguished professor of Cornell University, on "Mac-Carthy's Translations of Calderon".

THE DIVINE PHILOTHEA.

An Auto.

"'The Divine Philothea', probably the last work of the kind written by Calderon, and as such worthy of attention, inasmuch as it is the composition of an old man of eighty-one, is conceived with much boldness and executed with marvellous skill. No fewer than twenty personages are represented on the stage, and these have their several parts allotted to them with great discrimination, ingenuity, and judgment. The Senses, the Cardinal Virtues; Paganism and Judaism; Heresy and Atheism; the Prince of Light and the Power of Darkness, figure amongst the characters".

"The Bookseller", June 29, 1867, on Mac-Carthy's "Mysteries of Corpus Christi (Autos Sacramentales), from the Spanish of Calderon".

THE TWO LOVERS OF HEAVEN.

A Drama.

"Of these 'The Wonder-working Magician' is most celebrated; but others, as 'The Joseph of Women', 'The Two Lovers of Heaven', quite deserve to be placed on a level if not higher than it. A tender pathetic grace is shed over this last, which gives it a peculiar charm".

Archbishop Trench.

Calderon's Autos Sacramentales, or Mysteries of Corpus Christi. Duffy: Dublin and London, 1867.

From "The Irish Ecclesiastical Record".

"In conclusion, we heartily commend to our readers this most interesting and valuable specimen of Spanish thought and devotion, wrought, as it is, into such pure and beautiful English. . . . . When we remember the great literary advantages which Spain once possessed in the intellect and faith of her literary giants, we may well rejoice in the appearance among us of one of the greatest of that noble race in the person of Calderon, especially when introduced to us by a poet whose claim upon our consideration has been so emphatically made good by his own original productions as Denis Florence Mac-Carthy".

THE SPANISH DRAMA

Just ready, double columns, price 2s. 6d.,

THE TWO LOVERS OF HEAVEN,

From the Spanish of Calderon,
BY DENIS FLORENCE MAC-CARTHY,

Author of The Voyage of St. Brendan, The Bell-Founder, Waiting for the May, etc.

DUBLIN: W. B. KELLY, 8 GRAFTON STREET.

BY THE SAME AUTHOR.

In one vol. small 4to, double columns, with the Spanish text, beautifully printed by Whittingham, Price 7s. 6d.,

THREE DRAMAS OF CALDERON,

FROM THE SPANISH,
BY DENIS FLORENCE MAC-CARTHY.

From Ticknor's History of Spanish Literature.

"It is, I think, one of the boldest attempts ever made in English verse. It is, too, as it seems to me, remarkably successful . . .

"Nothing, I think, in the English language will give us so true an impression of what is most characteristic of the Spanish drama: perhaps I ought to say, of what is most characteristic of Spanish poetry generally".--tom. iii. pp. 461, 462.

BERNARD QUARITCH, 15 PICCADILLY, LONDON.

Transcriber's Notes.

General. I have rendered instances of small capitals as all capitals. In most instances I have made no attempt to indicate here instances of italics in the original publication. Accents and other diacritical marks have also been dropt. However, where the original has an acute accent over the "e" in a past participle for poetical reasons, I have marked this with a grave accent (as in "learn`ed") to indicate the intended pronunciation. For a fully formatted version, with italics, extended characters, et cetera, please refer to the HTML version of this play, released by Project Gutenberg simultaneously with this plain text edition.

General. Only the most obvious of printer's errors have been corrected in this electronic edition. Some inconsistent use of quotation marks and several forms of ellipses (with varying numbers of dots and spaces) have been retained as originally published. I have also retained the original's format of contractions, namely to include a space as in "I 'll" rather than "I'll."

Play, General. Stage directions following lines of spoken text are typically right justified in the printed source. In this electronic edition they simply follow the line of spoken text.

Play, General. In a few places, Denis Florence MacCarthy's (1817-1882) translation as published differs noticeably from a Spanish (or more properly, Castillano) text of the drama, published after this translation, available to this transcriber. I do not have access to the Spanish edition that Mr. MacCarthy used as the basis of his translation, so perhaps a better preserved version of Pedro Calderon de la Barca's (1600-1681) drama was discovered. Or perhaps Mr. MacCarthy used some poetic license in editing the drama. Some differences may be due to printer's errors. Whatever the reason, I have noted below these differences so that a reader comparing this e-book to a Spanish edition will not be confused about these omission, and think them caused by a transcription error of mine, or pages missing from the printed source.

Act 1, Scene 2. Ovid's 'Remedy of Love' is referred to three times, but as 'Remedies of Love' on the third occasion. A Spanish text has "Remedio" the first time, and "Remedios" elsewhere. I have found references to the work as both 'Remedium Amoris' and 'Remedia Amoris.'

Act 1, Scene 2. There is an apparent discrepancy in the play. Chloris is clearly present in the grove, and in "Persons" is listed as one of four priestesses of Diana, yet the lines "We three share;--'t is thy delight" and "For here three objects we behold" imply she is not part of the group of priestesses. There is no stage direction [such as: (Chloris sits behind a tree.] in the printed source, nor in a Spanish text of the play, to explain this. Perhaps (as may be guessed from the line "From their tender years go thither" in the previous scene) the character is an acolyte or novice priestess played by a child. She only appears in this scene.

Act 1, Scene 2. "My blessings on your choice and you! / . . . Are nothing to a pretty face." A Spanish text gives Escarpin seventeen lines here, rather than five. The last dozen lines contain a story of a clever vixen and a comely partridge.

Act 1, Scene 3. The line "Yes, God and Man is Christ" is not indented in the printed source, but logically should be, and is in a Spanish text of the play. I have indented it above.

Act 1, Scene 3. The line "Why delay? Arrest them." in the printed source is shown as two lines ("Why delay? / Arrest them."), but this seems to be a printer's error as it breaks the asonante verse pattern.

Act 1, Scene 3. In order to preserve the verse, I have indented the line "Why, why, O heavens!"

Act 2, Scene 1. I have indented the line "What then?"

Act 2, Scene 1. With the line "Clemency in fine had won," there is another apparent discrepancy in the play. Polemius is angry at Chrysanthus when the soldiers return in Act 1, Scene 3.

Act 2, Scene 3. In the line "Here the jasmin doubly white," the word jasmine is spelt without an "e."

Act 2, Scene 3. In Nisida's song, in the line "The bless`ed rapture of forgetting", the printed source has "blessed" without an accent on the second "e." Because this line is repeated twice more in the scene with the accent, I have added it to this first instance in the text above.

Act 2, Scene 3. The printed source lists Escarpin as the speaker of the lines "My lord, oh! hearken / To my song once more." A Spanish text indicates that Nisida speaks here, as is only logical, so I have listed Nisida as speaker in the text above.

Act 2, Scene 3. There seems to be a gap in the dialog after "Not myself, no aid is granted." A Spanish text has four additional lines here: [D.] Luego tu tan de su parte / Estas, que a ellos los ensalzas? / [C.] Si; que he visto muchas cosas / Hoy en mi favor obradas.

Act 3, Scene 1. In a Spanish text, after the line "I could listen to such nonsense?" Escarpin has five lines of monolog.

Act 3, Scene 1. In a Spanish text the line "Whence did sound the voice?" is spoken by Chrysanthus, which would naturally agree with Polemius' reply to Chrysanthus immediately below. Also, just before this line, Chrysanthus says: Sin mi me ha dejado a mi.

Act 3, Scene 1. In the line "The two lover saints of Heaven." the phrase "lover saints" is not hyphenated, although the same phrase is hyphenated just before the end of the play. The Spanish text has "Los dos amantes del cielo" in both places.

Act 3, Scene 1. After the line "The two lover saints of Heaven." there are forty lines of dialog between Escarpin and Polemius. In typical Escarpine style, it contains a story. Here is a free translation: A man is on trial for killing his father and loving his mother. The judge berates the lawyer, "How dare you defend a man who has committed the worst possible crime." The lawyer replies, "I disagree, your Honor, for to kill his mother and love his father would, indeed, have been a worse crime."

Act 3, Scene 2. There is a break in the asonante verse at the line "They the open country seek".

Act 3, Scene 2. In the line "So part pagan and part christian", near the end of the scene, Christian is not capitalized in the printed source.

Note 3. The scene actually ends on page 17 rather than 25 in the source publication. This page numbering problem also occurs in Note 12 and probably corresponds to a draught version of the publication--a detail not caught in the final editing. The last phrase of this note was actually printed: "the fu ll consonant rhyme." As no letters seem to logically fit in the empty space between "fu" and "ll," I have replaced this with the word "full" in the text above.

Note 12. This refers to Note 5, which is actually on page 12 in the source publication, rather than page 21.

Note 13. The Spanish text in the section of the drama noted is in five-lined stanzas. However, although Mr. MacCarthy's English generally follows that metre here, he does break the format in a several places.

www.bookjungle.com *email:* sales@bookjungle.com *fax:* 630-214-0564 *mail: Book Jungle PO Box 2226 Champaign, IL 61825*

The Codes Of Hammurabi And Moses
W. W. Davies

QTY

The discovery of the Hammurabi Code is one of the greatest achievements of archaeology, and is of paramount interest, not only to the student of the Bible, but also to all those interested in ancient history...

Religion **ISBN:** *1-59462-338-4* **Pages:** 132 *MSRP $12.95*

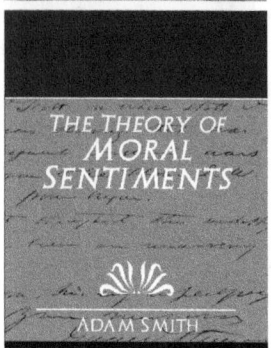

The Theory of Moral Sentiments
Adam Smith

QTY

This work from 1749. contains original theories of conscience amd moral judgment and it is the foundation for systemof morals.

Philosophy **ISBN:** *1-59462-777-0* **Pages:** 536 *MSRP $19.95*

Jessica's First Prayer
Hesba Stretton

QTY

In a screened and secluded corner of one of the many railway-bridges which span the streets of London there could be seen a few years ago, from five o'clock every morning until half past eight, a tidily set-out coffee-stall, consisting of a trestle and board, upon which stood two large tin cans, with a small fire of charcoal burning under each so as to keep the coffee boiling during the early hours of the morning when the work-people were thronging into the city on their way to their daily toil...

Childrens **ISBN:** *1-59462-373-2* **Pages:** 84 *MSRP $9.95*

My Life and Work
Henry Ford

QTY

Henry Ford revolutionized the world with his implementation of mass production for the Model T automobile. Gain valuable business insight into his life and work with his own auto-biography... "We have only started on our development of our country we have not as yet, with all our talk of wonderful progress, done more than scratch the surface. The progress has been wonderful enough but..."

Biographies/ **ISBN:** *1-59462-198-5* **Pages:** 300 *MSRP $21.95*

www.bookjungle.com email: sales@bookjungle.com fax: 630-214-0564 mail: Book Jungle PO Box 2226 Champaign, IL 61825

The Art of Cross-Examination
Francis Wellman

I presume it is the experience of every author, after his first book is published upon an important subject, to be almost overwhelmed with a wealth of ideas and illustrations which could readily have been included in his book, and which to his own mind, at least, seem to make a second edition inevitable. Such certainly was the case with me; and when the first edition had reached its sixth impression in five months, I rejoiced to learn that it seemed to my publishers that the book had met with a sufficiently favorable reception to justify a second and considerably enlarged edition. ..

QTY

Reference   ISBN: *1-59462-647-2*   Pages:412 MSRP *$19.95*

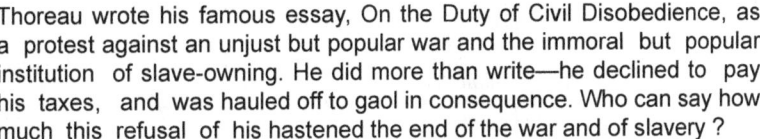

On the Duty of Civil Disobedience
Henry David Thoreau

Thoreau wrote his famous essay, On the Duty of Civil Disobedience, as a protest against an unjust but popular war and the immoral but popular institution of slave-owning. He did more than write—he declined to pay his taxes, and was hauled off to gaol in consequence. Who can say how much this refusal of his hastened the end of the war and of slavery?

QTY

Law   ISBN: *1-59462-747-9*   Pages:48 MSRP *$7.45*

Dream Psychology Psychoanalysis for Beginners
Sigmund Freud

Sigmund Freud, born Sigismund Schlomo Freud (May 6, 1856 - September 23, 1939), was a Jewish-Austrian neurologist and psychiatrist who co-founded the psychoanalytic school of psychology. Freud is best known for his theories of the unconscious mind, especially involving the mechanism of repression; his redefinition of sexual desire as mobile and directed towards a wide variety of objects; and his therapeutic techniques, especially his understanding of transference in the therapeutic relationship and the presumed value of dreams as sources of insight into unconscious desires.

QTY

Psychology   ISBN: *1-59462-905-6*   Pages:196 MSRP *$15.45*

The Miracle of Right Thought
Orison Swett Marden

Believe with all of your heart that you will do what you were made to do. When the mind has once formed the habit of holding cheerful, happy, prosperous pictures, it will not be easy to form the opposite habit. It does not matter how improbable or how far away this realization may see, or how dark the prospects may be, if we visualize them as best we can, as vividly as possible, hold tenaciously to them and vigorously struggle to attain them, they will gradually become actualized, realized in the life. But a desire, a longing without endeavor, a yearning abandoned or held indifferently will vanish without realization.

QTY

Self Help   ISBN: *1-59462-644-8*   Pages:360 MSRP *$25.45*

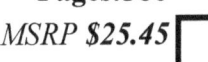

www.bookjungle.com email: sales@bookjungle.com fax: 630-214-0564 mail: Book Jungle PO Box 2226 Champaign, IL 61825

QTY

	Title	ISBN	Price
☐	**The Rosicrucian Cosmo-Conception Mystic Christianity** by *Max Heindel*	1-59462-188-8	$38.95
	The Rosicrucian Cosmo-conception is not dogmatic, neither does it appeal to any other authority than the reason of the student. It is: not controversial, but is: sent forth in the, hope that it may help to clear...	New Age/Religion Pages 646	
☐	**Abandonment To Divine Providence** by *Jean-Pierre de Caussade*	1-59462-228-0	$25.95
	"The Rev. Jean Pierre de Caussade was one of the most remarkable spiritual writers of the Society of Jesus in France in the 18th Century. His death took place at Toulouse in 1751. His works have gone through many editions and have been republished...	Inspirational/Religion Pages 400	
☐	**Mental Chemistry** by *Charles Haanel*	1-59462-192-6	$23.95
	Mental Chemistry allows the change of material conditions by combining and appropriately utilizing the power of the mind. Much like applied chemistry creates something new and unique out of careful combinations of chemicals the mastery of mental chemistry...	New Age Pages 354	
☐	**The Letters of Robert Browning and Elizabeth Barret Barrett 1845-1846 vol II** by *Robert Browning* and *Elizabeth Barrett*	1-59462-193-4	$35.95
		Biographies Pages 596	
☐	**Gleanings In Genesis (volume I)** by *Arthur W. Pink*	1-59462-130-6	$27.45
	Appropriately has Genesis been termed "the seed plot of the Bible" for in it we have, in germ form, almost all of the great doctrines which are afterwards fully developed in the books of Scripture which follow...	Religion/Inspirational Pages 420	
☐	**The Master Key** by *L. W. de Laurence*	1-59462-001-6	$30.95
	In no branch of human knowledge has there been a more lively increase of the spirit of research during the past few years than in the study of Psychology, Concentration and Mental Discipline. The requests for authentic lessons in Thought Control, Mental Discipline and...	New Age/Business Pages 422	
☐	**The Lesser Key Of Solomon Goetia** by *L. W. de Laurence*	1-59462-092-X	$9.95
	This translation of the first book of the "Lernegton" which is now for the first time made accessible to students of Talismanic Magic was done, after careful collation and edition, from numerous Ancient Manuscripts in Hebrew, Latin, and French...	New Age/Occult Pages 92	
☐	**Rubaiyat Of Omar Khayyam** by *Edward Fitzgerald*	1-59462-332-5	$13.95
	Edward Fitzgerald, whom the world has already learned, in spite of his own efforts to remain within the shadow of anonymity, to look upon as one of the rarest poets of the century, was born at Bredfield, in Suffolk, on the 31st of March, 1809. He was the third son of John Purcell...	Music Pages 172	
☐	**Ancient Law** by *Henry Maine*	1-59462-128-4	$29.95
	The chief object of the following pages is to indicate some of the earliest ideas of mankind, as they are reflected in Ancient Law, and to point out the relation of those ideas to modern thought.	Religiom/History Pages 452	
☐	**Far-Away Stories** by *William J. Locke*	1-59462-250-7	$19.45
	"Good wine needs no bush, but a collection of mixed vintages does. And this book is just such a collection. Some of the stories I do not want to remain buried for ever in the museum files of dead magazine-numbers an author's not unpardonable vanity..."	Fiction Pages 272	
☐	**Life of David Crockett** by *David Crockett*	1-59462-129-2	$27.45
	"Colonel David Crockett was one of the most remarkable men of the times in which he lived. Born in humble life, but gifted with a strong will, an indomitable courage, and unremitting perseverance...	Biographies/New Age Pages 424	
☐	**Lip-Reading** by *Edward Nitchie*	1-59462-206-X	$25.95
	Edward B. Nitchie, founder of the New York School for the Hard of Hearing, now the Nitchie School of Lip-Reading, Inc, wrote "LIP-READING Principles and Practice". The development and perfecting of this meritorious work on lip-reading was an undertaking...	How-to Pages 400	
☐	**A Handbook of Suggestive Therapeutics, Applied Hypnotism, Psychic Science** by *Henry Munro*	1-59462-214-0	$24.95
		Health/New Age/Health/Self-help Pages 376	
☐	**A Doll's House: and Two Other Plays** by *Henrik Ibsen*	1-59462-112-8	$19.95
	Henrik Ibsen created this classic when in revolutionary 1848 Rome. Introducing some striking concepts in playwriting for the realist genre, this play has been studied the world over.	Fiction/Classics/Plays 308	
☐	**The Light of Asia** by *sir Edwin Arnold*	1-59462-204-3	$13.95
	In this poetic masterpiece, Edwin Arnold describes the life and teachings of Buddha. The man who was to become known as Buddha to the world was born as Prince Gautama of India but he rejected the worldly riches and abandoned the reigns of power when...	Religion/History/Biographies Pages 170	
☐	**The Complete Works of Guy de Maupassant** by *Guy de Maupassant*	1-59462-157-8	$16.95
	"For days and days, nights and nights, I had dreamed of that first kiss which was to consecrate our engagement, and I knew not on what spot I should put my lips..."	Fiction/Classics Pages 240	
☐	**The Art of Cross-Examination** by *Francis L. Wellman*	1-59462-309-0	$26.95
	Written by a renowned trial lawyer, Wellman imparts his experience and uses case studies to explain how to use psychology to extract desired information through questioning.	How-to/Science/Reference Pages 408	
☐	**Answered or Unanswered?** by *Louisa Vaughan* Miracles of Faith in China	1-59462-248-5	$10.95
		Religion Pages 112	
☐	**The Edinburgh Lectures on Mental Science (1909)** by *Thomas*	1-59462-008-3	$11.95
	This book contains the substance of a course of lectures recently given by the writer in the Queen Street Hall, Edinburgh. Its purpose is to indicate the Natural Principles governing the relation between Mental Action and Material Conditions...	New Age/Psychology Pages 148	
☐	**Ayesha** by *H. Rider Haggard*	1-59462-301-5	$24.95
	Verily and indeed it is the unexpected that happens! Probably if there was one person upon the earth from whom the Editor of this, and of a certain previous history, did not expect to hear again...	Classics Pages 380	
☐	**Ayala's Angel** by *Anthony Trollope*	1-59462-352-X	$29.95
	The two girls were both pretty, but Lucy who was twenty-one who supposed to be simple and comparatively unattractive, whereas Ayala was credited, as her Bombwhat romantic name might show, with poetic charm and a taste for romance. Ayala when her father died was nineteen...	Fiction Pages 484	
☐	**The American Commonwealth** by *James Bryce*	1-59462-286-8	$34.45
	An interpretation of American democratic political theory. It examines political mechanics and society from the perspective of Scotsman James Bryce	Politics Pages 572	
☐	**Stories of the Pilgrims** by *Margaret P. Pumphrey*	1-59462-116-0	$17.95
	This book explores pilgrims religious oppression in England as well as their escape to Holland and eventual crossing to America on the Mayflower, and their early days in New England...	History Pages 268	

www.bookjungle.com *email: sales@bookjungle.com fax:* 630-214-0564 *mail:* Book Jungle PO Box 2226 Champaign, IL 61825

QTY

The Fasting Cure *by Sinclair Upton* ISBN: *1-59462-222-1* $13.95
In the Cosmopolitan Magazine for May, 1910, and in the Contemporary Review (London) for April, 1910, I published an article dealing with my experiences in fasting. I have written a great many magazine articles, but never one which attracted so much attention... *New Age/Self Help/Health Pages 164*

Hebrew Astrology *by Sepharial* ISBN: *1-59462-308-2* $13.45
In these days of advanced thinking it is a matter of common observation that we have left many of the old landmarks behind and that we are now pressing forward to greater heights and to a wider horizon than that which represented the mind-content of our progenitors... *Astrology Pages 144*

Thought Vibration or The Law of Attraction in the Thought World ISBN: *1-59462-127-6* $12.95
by William Walker Atkinson *Psychology/Religion Pages 144*

Optimism *by Helen Keller* ISBN: *1-59462-108-X* $15.95
Helen Keller was blind, deaf, and mute since 19 months old, yet famously learned how to overcome these handicaps, communicate with the world, and spread her lectures promoting optimism. An inspiring read for everyone... *Biographies/Inspirational Pages 84*

Sara Crewe *by Frances Burnett* ISBN: *1-59462-360-0* $9.45
In the first place, Miss Minchin lived in London. Her home was a large, dull, tall one, in a large, dull square, where all the houses were alike, and all the sparrows were alike, and where all the door-knockers made the same heavy sound... *Childrens/Classic Pages 88*

The Autobiography of Benjamin Franklin *by Benjamin Franklin* ISBN: *1-59462-135-7* $24.95
The Autobiography of Benjamin Franklin has probably been more extensively read than any other American historical work, and no other book of its kind has had such ups and downs of fortune. Franklin lived for many years in England, where he was agent... *Biographies/History Pages 332*

Name	
Email	
Telephone	
Address	
City, State ZIP	

☐ Credit Card   ☐ Check / Money Order

Credit Card Number	
Expiration Date	
Signature	

Please Mail to: Book Jungle
PO Box 2226
Champaign, IL 61825
or Fax to: 630-214-0564

ORDERING INFORMATION

web: *www.bookjungle.com*
email: *sales@bookjungle.com*
fax: *630-214-0564*
mail: *Book Jungle PO Box 2226 Champaign, IL 61825*
or PayPal *to sales@bookjungle.com*

Please contact us for bulk discounts

DIRECT-ORDER TERMS

20% Discount if You Order Two or More Books
Free Domestic Shipping!
Accepted: Master Card, Visa, Discover, American Express

www.ingramcontent.com/pod-product-compliance
Lightning Source LLC
Chambersburg PA
CBHW081836170426
43199CB00017B/2745